NARCISSUS

NARCISSUS

BY ARIEL TSAI

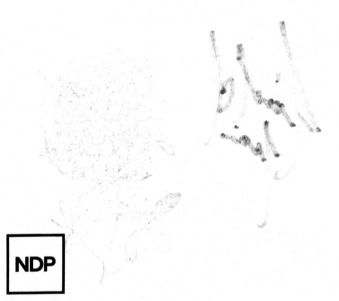

NDP

NEW DEGREE PRESS

NARCISSUS

ISBN   978-1-63730-655-0 *Paperback*

978-1-63730-738-0 *Kindle Ebook*

978-1-63730-929-2 *Ebook*

Contents

Author's Note

———

forget talking about sex: I wish
someone had sat me down when I was younger to tell
my unformed self you do not have to be anything. love
is not transactional conditional contractual.
your voice is worth hearing and you do not have to be anything.
you do not have to be good. your voice is worth hearing.
you do not have to be good. you are worth loving.

(FROM *QUOTA*, PAGE 197)

I have always been and still am an incredibly self-conscious person, in the sense of being overly conscious of myself to the point of mortification. Since identity is an eternally fluctuating work in progress, *who am I* was a persistently urgent and perpetually unanswerable question of mine from early on. That kind of instability can be frightening for a lonely, anxious child, so I sought to make sense of myself and my thoughts in terms of words.

The power of language—to create, to connect, to empower—has always fascinated me, as has its structure and sociocultural significance. The fact that English, my chosen artistic medium, is my native language but not my first language is metaphorically significant, I think. A lot of inane things have metaphorical significance to me because I, like so many others, suffer from the desire for my life to be meaningful. Maybe that's why my thoughts so often take shape in poetry, wherein even the most mundane aspects of life and language and poetic structure can and do have significance.

Language and the world are both such big, unwieldy things, and yet through poetry, I can wield them just a little. The artist is a little god, shaping their little pieces of the world in their own image. When you can quantify the world around you and see familiar faces (and whose face is more familiar than your own?) from time to time as a result of your work, it is a comfort. And so I write poetry.

Poetry was something I turned to as a preteen struggling with the onset of chronic depression on top of all the normal woes of growing up: questioning my sexuality, grappling with my identity as a Taiwanese American, wondering if anything I ever did was going to matter if the Sun or climate crisis or natural disaster was going to swallow the Earth someday anyway, etcetera. I felt desperately alone so much of the time. I wrote this book because it's the kind of book I wish I had encountered as a teenager: something that put what I was feeling into words, that could quantify these things that felt so awful and confusing and all-consuming.

I wrote this book, in other words, for myself. It's not called *Narcissus* for nothing. But if it truly was written for me and me alone, what would be the point in publishing? To publish, there must be an audience in mind. So who am I thinking about? Who am I writing for? You, of course. You who feel alone in your grief or your anger or your fear. You whose trauma seems to be crushing you. You who are questioning yourself. You who are exploring yourself. You who are creating yourself. I hope it can make you feel at least a little less alone. My journey is my own, yes, but maybe you can see your own reflection in parts of it.

This collection is named after Narcissus, the Greek youth immortalized in Ovid's *Metamorphoses*, known for his fatal love for himself. This sort of thing—writing something and deciding it's worth sharing with the world—is always a bit of a narcissistic endeavor. Not that that's necessarily a bad thing. I think most writing is an exercise of self-portraiture to one degree or another, since we can only write what we know and we can only know through the lens of our own perspective.

We are all too often trapped in our own solipsistic worlds, unable to truly connect with one another, a state of affairs that impedes understanding and stifles empathy. Lack of empathy is the key issue behind many of our society's problems. It leads to misunderstandings, stereotyping, discrimination, and oppression. It leads to seeing other human beings as less than oneself and thus justifies their exploitation. Literature—what I spent my years as an undergraduate studying, and a lifetime loving—allows us to catch a glimpse into the soul of another in a way that nothing else can. It helps us understand the experiences of others. Regardless of genre, good literature lights a fire in the mind of the reader which burns away ignorance and shapes how they see and engage with the world from then on.

This book you have here in your hands is a piece of my soul: my message in a bottle, thrown out to sea. It catalogues what I found in my exploratory journey through the uncharted depths of myself. I'd ask you to be careful with it, but I don't think I need to. I'm sure you're able to feel the pulse of my thoughts through these pages too, and most people are good about being gentle to the little lives in their hands.

My therapist says I have trouble with vulnerability, because vulnerability takes trust, and trust in others is something I all too often struggle with.

If I put my little glass house of a heart in someone else's hands, who's to say they won't drop it, unintentionally or otherwise? But I've been working on that, and on the rest of me too. This book has been a part of that process. If the eyes are the windows to the soul, then this book is a skylight or a glass wall. It's as vulnerable as it gets.

I'm afraid, of course. But here I am. Perhaps me being brave about my vulnerability will make it easier for you to do the same. To tell your story and make your voice heard. To help people understand and empathize with you and people like you. Because of course you're not alone. And of course, you are worth being heard, and you are worth being loved. All it takes is for you to be a little braver.

Warning: This book contains occasional mentions, frank discussions, and overwrought contemplations of topics which may be sensitive for some readers. These include but are not limited to mental illness, suicide, death, violence, abuse, and trauma. There is an appendix at the end of the book which has more details on which poems contain these sensitive themes for those who wish either to emotionally prepare themselves for or to entirely avoid said poems.

This book also rather unfortunately contains gratuitous use of multisyllabic words which are usually only acceptable in standardized testing, extensive classical and religious imagery, and concepts which ought to have remained within the firm bounds of a Philosophy 101 seminar. The author thinks at least most of it is tasteful enough but is also aware of her tendencies towards insensitive bluntness and towards beating the dead horse of a metaphor beyond even the hope of reincarnation to get every last damn *inch* she can out of it, so she sees fit to warn you. There is no appendix cataloging these crimes, however. The entirety of the book is rife with it. *Caveat emptor*, indeed.

As for the content of this collection, some of this is fiction, but all of it is truth. Names, characters, businesses, events, and incidents may or may not be the products of the author's imagination. Any resemblance to actual persons, living or dead, or actual events may or may not be coincidental. Read at your own risk.

I

"... she asked the seer,
Would he long years and ripe old age enjoy,
Who answered 'If he shall himself not know.'"

- OVID, METAMORPHOSES

(TRANSLATED BY A.D. MELVILLE)

origins

my past which no longer inhabits me (or does it?).

i

in my mind's eye, I am standing
in the driveway of my childhood home. looking up at
the stripped eaves quivering in the sweet air
and the blue haze of suburban twilight.
listening to the sounds of my past
echoing in the empty street.
sometimes, I struggle to articulate,
my thoughts moving like flies in syrup,
we were almost happy here.

but do I remember anymore?
(did you have dimples on both sides?
or just one? the color of your eyes so unsure.)
my present with its filthy fingers and
filthier mouth has dirtied my past,
coloring it in with a hazy patina:
ash gray. mourning white.
the black-blue-yellow of aging bruises.

ii

therapists and lovers alike try
to plumb my depths, looking for all the world like
children digging aimlessly in the sand
with all the importance and gravitas youthful naivete
(god, you were so young)
gives an unimportant task.

iii

my own childhood is a story which has
been told to me, not a memory I own or know
except in the silent, twitching fibers of my muscles
and the raw endings of my ever-vigilant nerves,
which startle as the call of a train a mile of night away
rumbles, shaking my childhood room (as if
expecting something awful at all times;

who taught them that? who taught me to
hold my breath when passing through graveyards,
to fear the shadows solicitous and sirenic?)

I'm not afraid of you, though.
nor was I afraid for you.
I never was. you never gave me cause to fear.

which was why afterwards I was left
searching desperately through the moth-eaten
photo-film of my memory, looking for a sign.
perhaps a smile that didn't quite blaze its way
across your entire face (lighting you up
like the sun. like always. so bright it hurt.
but how could I ever look away?)
the starlight missing from your eyes, perhaps.
what color were they again? blue? gray?
storm?ash?cerulean?green?thunderhead?sky blue?

blue as your lips:
was there something I had missed?

V

sometimes I think about the baby sparrow
whose heart stopped out of fear
which we buried in the backyard so many years ago.
so small its whole body shook with its pulse,
speeding towards failure as we godlike looked on.
(I wonder: as you died, struggling to breathe,
were you afraid of the leap you'd taken into the unknown?)
I still dream some nights about its hollow bones
being unearthed by rain. it was the first thing
I ever watched die. for years after,

whenever I found myself gasping
for breath, being pulled out to sea
by the riptide of my panic, I would wonder
if that was how I too would die:
bones and pericardium shaking apart with terror
and god as my silent bystander.
but it's been so long now, generations of sparrows late
rising and falling with the wind, their hollow skeletons

surely lost by now to the roots of new life.
they say in ten years all of the cells in your body
have been reborn, that you are the same and other.
(you are still the same, still hanging in your closet:
a time capsule of a person of a ghost, frozen unbreathing in place.
the whole time I knew you: was I watching you die?)

I am older now than you have ever been. will ever be.

not a cell in my body now knows you.

(would you even recognize me?)

~~my sparrow my butterfly~~ my friend,

have your bones fed the trees yet?

妖怪

妖怪 *yāoguài: (n.) monster, demon. Literally, "strange ghost/monster."*

one of my earliest memories is of an uncle who was not my uncle
telling me why I should fear the wind: planting the seeds of
nightmares about eyes in the windows and the searching hands
of the hungry ghosts and dead men walking,
their crying voices the substance of the stormy air (hold your breath),
groaning under the weight of their bloated emptiness and
of damnation eternal as penance for their crimes in life and death.

be a good girl, I was told, (and if you can't do that, at least progenate)
so that there will be offerings at your grave
to sate your undying dead hunger (and someone left to bury you).
either breed or perish(or unperish forever), for no one will pray for you
if you do not make them
make themselves bury you well and

satiate you out of fearful(hold your breath)respect
and/or the vague hope of their own progeny following
the same worn paths of tradition winding through generations of lifetimes
of so many strange ghosts, moaning in the night.

bloodborne

i

we were born at the same time in queens but you
died first, and afterwards my family moved
out to the suburbs. when your parents moved in next door,
they planted a garden.

you died and then your mother tried to teach me about plants
because she couldn't teach you because you're one of the examples
of things people point out to prove that even if God is real,
he's cruel or silent or impotent (why else would childhood cancer exist?)
and we couldn't find anyone who could fit
in your skin in your blood in your bones
I'm sorry I couldn't fit and that I still can't tell
where or when I should prune the roses and that I still
can't fit and that I, in childlike cruelty,
complained when she tried to teach me how to tell when tomatoes are ripe.

I'm living on borrowed time even though
my blood and bones and contents of my skin is my own
but there's a cancer that's not a cancer eating through
my brain and my heart and my self and
that's why I'm so self-centered so preoccupied with myself and
I'm sorry I'm sorry I'm sorry I'm so
ungrateful for my borrowed time and sometimes I wish you could
take it back; I've lived a dozen of your lifetimes
and have never felt I deserved them.

I can't fit in my skin and that's why I tried so many times
to let the blood out let the ghosts out let
the cancer that isn't cancer but is still a sleeping dragon under my skin out
out in ladder track lines up my arms and thighs and hips
out with the rocks in my pockets and the air from my protesting lungs
out with a chair kicked over and no note;

ii

where is your grave now, I wonder?

I sometimes weep when I see baby shoes (not for sale,

they've been worn) because they're just so goddamn small

and death just always seems like it happens to other people. older people.

do they make baby coffins? are you buried in the city where we once lived?

I can't remember your face anymore, and my childhood photos have been

lost to parental division. but what would it matter anyway?

do the dead even stay put?

or has your ghost followed your parents out to the suburbs?

I think only god can forgive you, only
god is dead, strangled on a mouthful of cliche
(divine mortality notwithstanding, I do still pray sometimes.
not for you or even for me, but because
it can't hurt. can it?), so I suppose
you're fresh out of luck.
I'd say I'm sorry. but you did not raise me
to be a liar.

of course I hope your soul finds peace *somewhere*.
I'd just rather it be somewhere far away from me.

wicked game

the empty-eyed house I grew up in,
with its cold hands and mess of a heart
languishing in the suburban streetlight,
holds no appeal for me, what with
my relinquished childhood lying on its side
in the front yard. bleeding out.

it's a game of clue, and this is the result.
so what's the solution?
remember: [perpetrator]
in the [place]
with a [weapon].
give your answers now.

perhaps: father
in the bedroom
with a smiling mouth and unsmiling eyes

or: god (silent)
in the bedroom
with father dearest keeping his hands to myself

or: therapist
in his office
with the insistence father dearest did nothing wrong

or: mother
in the middle of a weepful conversation
with her inability/unwillingness/unincentive to believe

whatever the case, the ending is the same:
I'm alone in the room with him and
my childhood tries to flee the cage of
my house so she opens the window and
punches out the screen and
jumps, forgetting that
her wings were clipped years ago:
hanging in the air for a moment before
gravity pulls her irresistibly down
into the waiting arms of the front yard.

you are me.

i

you have a bad day. you have a bad day. you have a bad day. you have so many bad days in a row that you forget what a good day is like. your measure for what is considered a good day is no longer the same; you have lowered your expectations a great deal. and yet you still keep having bad days.

ii

you do not fear ghosts until it is dark and you are alone and there is no one left to laugh at your fear. (fear is the mind-killer and you are being driven out of it: your mind. your fear.) you want to creep out of bed and light a cigarette so it can keep your shaking hands company, but the shadows are watching you. your breathing taunts them. they are watching you.

iii

oftentimes when an animal is aggressive, it is actually afraid. so what are you afraid of? and why does it make you bite at the few hands which still dare to feed you? (of course you're lonely. but most of the time it doesn't even matter to you. you're just lonely. it is a fact of life. it is your fault. of course you're lonely. it doesn't matter.)

iv

you have a bad day. you think about killing yourself. you have a bad day. you think about killing yourself. you have a not-so-bad day, and you still think about killing yourself. you don't really want to kill yourself (you think) and yet you are still thinking about it. it is the scab you cannot stop picking at.

vi

you have a bad day. like many of your bad days, that means you don't get much done, and what little you do get done feels trite. it means your veins are full of lead and every goddamn thing takes so much god-damn energy and you haven't taken a goddamn shower in four fucking days because it's been four fucking bad days in a row and you're just so fucking tired. it's a bad day and you're so fucking tired. it's a bad day and you think about killing yourself but that would mean having to fucking get up and so you don't. it's a bad day and you just want to sleep until the day is over and then maybe, just maybe, if you're really lucky (which you rarely are), tomorrow won't be such a bad day.

viii

you think about killing yourself a lot for someone who doesn't want
to die, and maybe it should concern you more than it does. but you
only think about killing yourself as a possible solution to any problem because it is one. don't want to finish that paper? you could kill
yourself. too much credit card debt? you could kill yourself. dog just
took a shit on your antique rug? you could kill yourself: and so on and
so forth. it's always a possibility, a glowing exit sign in your peripheral
vision. you still haven't left, because so far you've always been able to
find other, better solutions to your problems, solutions which don't
close off all of your other possibilities forever. you think about killing
yourself because it's just a possible solution, one possible solution. if
there's a situation in which it's the only possible solution, you haven't
found it yet.

the enemy(?)

i

statistically speaking you are more likely to die
at the hands of a loved one than a stranger's.
the ones who love you know you. they know so many of your
soft spots and secret places. they know where you hide
when the thunder frightens you and where you sleep.
who knows you better than them?

yourself, of course. you know
all your soft spots secret spaces hiding places.
you know the weak heel, the heated wax, the apple
and the serpent. what are the chances that you'll die
by your own hand? which way are the odds stacked?
which way would look more in your favor?

statistically speaking you are more likely to die
at the hands of a loved one. statistically speaking
you are more likely to die at your own hand
than that of someone else's.
funny, isn't it? the ways we show we love someone?

ii

my therapist says I have issues with control.
a manifestation of anxiety. of childhood trauma.
of not being able to say no and of not being able to trust
my memories. myself. anyone else.
needing to feel the sharp edges of my own agency in my white-knuckled grip.
I think I smell blood.

I read a self help book once that said
you cannot control the world.
you cannot control what happens to you.
you cannot control what cards you are dealt.
you can only control yourself.

you can control how you think about things.
how you see things. how you react to things.
the choices you make.
how your hand is played.
you can control yourself.

my therapist: *why are you so afraid of losing control?*
in my chest, it twists: the grief, that nameless creature,
murmuring in its restless sleep as it turns over.
I feel it there, twined around my aorta. breathing.
squeezing slightly as it moves. constricting.
growing. the pressure in my chest cavity increasing.
I don't want to hurt anyone. my voice is sodden with the moisture of despair.
she frowns. *you wouldn't do that.*
I smile a little, mirthless. *there's more than one way to hurt someone.*

I think of my sister, crying over the phone.
the twenty pounds I lost. the scars I gained.
the people I love. statistical likelihoods.
a grave with my name on it. waiting.
my hypothetical mother weeping before it.
the creature stirs. I bite down on my lip. I think I taste blood.
am I in control?

II

*"My joy! I see it; but the joy I see
I cannot find..."*

- OVID, METAMORPHOSES (TRANSLATED
BY A.D. MELVILLE)

白日依山盡

登鸛雀樓 *(dēngguànquèlóu): (n.)* "Climbing the Stork Tower," a poem by *Tang Dynasty poet Wang Zhihuan about the importance of perseverance and constant improvement. Like most other Tang* shi, *the poem is comprised of four lines, with five syllables each.*

up one floor more to
squint closer at the
white sun over the
mountains; the poem

a metaphor for
the burn in your thighs
and lungs and eyes when
you think your bones can

take you no further:
just up one floor more
(we are the builders
of great things: the wall,

the railroad (chinkchink)
so ignore the pain
the hunger heartache
sickness homesick hope

for something better
for your children, for
those you left behind,
an ocean away)

do not ask where the
stairs lead. do not ask
questions. we build for
others. do not ask

why. or who. or what
you are doing here
in the first place, your
face more sweat than skin,

climbing endlessly.
legs burning. but still
climbing. on and on.
ever upwards. know

the steps lead to the
top. that is enough.
do not ask what is
there. what is not there.

up one floor more, just
one floor more; the best
things come to those who
bite their tongues, wipe their

sweat, squint closer at
the white sun over
the mountains, then turn
back to the stairs; just

更上一層樓

The text of 登鸛雀樓:
白日依山盡, (báirìyīshānjìn)
黃河入海流; (huánghérùhǎiliú)
欲窮千里目, (yùqióngqiānlǐmù)
更上一層樓. (gèngshàngyīcénglóu)

Roughly translated:
The white sun sets behind the mountains,
and the Yellow River flows into the sea.

To see a thousand-mile view,
go up another floor.

dramaturgy

家醜不可外揚: *(idiom): Literally, "family shames must not be spread abroad." Essentially the same as the English idiom "don't air your dirty laundry in public."*

sociological dramaturgy: front stage first, backstage second.
here is your front stage self. here is your backstage self.
so often at odds. so long as the curtain is up, your mask is down.
the word *person* comes from the latin *persona*:
"an actor's mask, a character in a play." only later
would it come to mean "human being." in other words,
all the world is a stage, and
we are characters first. human second.
the show must go on. it does not matter if you are in pain.
the show must go on.

what we want is acceptance.
no: to 給自己面子, to save face,
not let ourselves our families 丟臉, lose face,
not let the audience see the ugliness through
a crack in the mask.

so. even in this house, there are things you do not speak.
the front door may be the entrance backstage,
but this performance does not end
just because you are no longer on stage. no.
so long as there are other people, there is an audience.
so long as there are other people, you wear a mask.
even around your fellow cast members.
other people. must not see. the show must go on.
the show must go on. it does not matter if you are in pain.

in this house, there are things you do not speak.

it does not matter if you are in pain. you do not speak
of the pain, of the shame. you do not speak,
and that is for the best. who would believe you anyway?
you are *just being lazy. need to try harder.*
go outside. stop moping. try harder.
are you even trying? you have nothing
to be sad about. I've sacrificed so much for you.
what are you even sad about, you ungrateful child?
it does not matter if it is not true. it does not matter
if you are in pain. you do not speak.

your pain does not matter. not even to you.

because even alone in your dressing room, you wear a mask.
you cannot take it off. you cannot be rid of it (丟臉?).
is it a mask? or is it your face? you cannot tell.
a persona or a person? you cannot tell.
is there a difference?
there are things you do not speak. even to yourself.
things which nobody should speak. outside or in.
front stage or back. it does not matter.
you do not speak of it, because you cannot.
because you do not. you have no vocabulary for it.

what is a person
if not a mask over a skeleton in the closet?
you are in pain, but it does not matter.
push it a little further under the rug.
in this house, there are things you do not speak.

crying wolf

once, when I was thirteen,
my father was paying for something.
the woman at the counter smiled at us and said something like
you and your girlfriend are beautiful together.
my father just smiled in response.

there are large parts of my childhood I do not/cannot/
will not/should not remember, particularly between
the ages of seven and fourteen. full chapters of my life
scribbled out, scribbled over.
left blank. my therapist says
it is a very common response to childhood trauma.
as are my periods of dissociation.
my overly ingrained startle reflex.
the early onset of severe, chronic clinical depression.

but I do remember that
for years, when my father physically expressed his affection,
the adrenaline would rush in:
~~flight~~ ~~fight~~ *freeze.* stiff and unresponsive
until he finally released me.

my mother once told me
there is a chinese saying that a daughter is
the incarnation of her father's wife in his past life.
that they loved each other so much in their past lives
that in this life, they wished to stay together.
as father and daughter. for some fucking reason.

so often, my father would tell me
I was making things up. imagining things.
lying. I was always lying, apparently.
the girl who cried wolf, crying wolf again.
this is why nobody ever believes you.
you're always lying. why are you always lying?

who would ever believe me?
I certainly was unsure of whether or not I could.
a lot of my childhood memories have a slightly
dreamlike quality to them. which is part of the reason
I have trouble believing they're real.
or maybe it's the doubt that colors them that way.

the girl who cried wolf sees what is maybe
a dog or a wolf and isn't sure what to do.
the girl who cried wolf has nightmares
for years about her father raping her.
sometimes she is her present self.
sometimes she is ten. eleven? she does not know.
sometimes he is only pressing the length of himself
against her back, and the dread paralyzes her.
nightmares or memories. she does not know.
how could she know. how could she know.

a wolf or a dog. a dog or a wolf.
crying in the night. or is that the voice of
her father's past wife, mourning?
how could she know. and
what difference would it make.
what could she do. who could ever believe her.

stockholm

i

in my dreams I tell you no and you still ignore me so I try to

push you away to fight you off but I'm

fighting underwater, my hits bearing little weight and the water

seeping into my lungs as I keep trying to tell you *no stop I said*

no please stop but you keep going and keep smiling and your smile changes

and I don't know which one you are anymore (why

have I let so many people take me apart/it's not my fault/but

why did I let them/not

my fault/) you keep smiling and ignoring me (in real life

you kept trying to convince me/why did I let you/not my fault/why

did I love you/not

my fault/)

I do not dream about rain; only fog, only

nothingness, the flatness of an expressionless winter sky

(are you smiling still? were you smiling then?

your always-smiling eyes not smiling now)

because so much depends on this silence, this weight:

my silence, under your weight between

my legs (/were it not for the silence I would

believe/it's not my fault/I wish I could hate/forget/forgive you/
but I remember you only
in my nighttime visions and my waking blindness, when I am
gagged and bound by the momentous burden of my body
and my love; my love, do you hear me
when I speak?)

ii

my nightmares borne of waking bruises
in the shape of your hands: your hand in
mine, your hands on mine, your hands on
     me. your hands in my mind, wandering. I loved you
          until I couldn't (I hate the parts of me that
          are you/that you made/that you gave
          me) until your hands on my skin
          made my nerves crawl over each other
in an attempt to escape your grasp

iii

there are days where I think I might resent you
for what you did to me. not just *that,*
but also the way you would talk circles around me
(*you're crazy*/*making things up*/am I/*you're*
always making things up/I am?)
        and sometimes I don't know what's real anymore
        if I dream(/nightmar)ed you and your hands and
not your hands (am I crazy? am I making things up?)

        and who would be able to tell me otherwise?
      my word against your word against me against reality

get out. get OUT.

at the shattered sound of my voice, the camera pans fast down to me having a panic attack on the floor by the foot of my bed in fetal position hands tangled in my hair and gasping gasping gasping and then up again to you just standing there to watch. the soundtrack is my ping pong thoughts and chopin etude op24no11 the piano descending and spiraling crescendoing spiraling spiraling as the left hand pounds pounds pounds all too too loud I cannot sleep I cannot breathe I cannot leave and you do not; the handheld camera shakes and I shake and all my molecules shake and we two observed collections of atoms are being behaviorally altered by the observation only there is no observer unless dr. eckleburg Himself silently ashily brooding counts but silent He is and silent I cannot be I cannot be I cannot be as I gasp gasp gasp for air oh god I'm dying oh god oh fuck. the camera pulls back to a wider angle as my tunnel vision closes in, the static from my limbs climbing through the bridges of my arteries and swimming through my nervous system to reach my head my heart my eyes oh god oh god I can't see oh god oh fuck. the camera watches and you watch me beg brokenly insanely for you to leave me be leave me alone leave me leave then pulls back in to a close up of your face darkened by nightfall and disappointment and perhaps the hope that this is not personal rapidly fading.

seasonally affective

the way my mood falls with the temperature and the leaves.

i

the summer sun supersaturating the colors in the trees,
peach and lilac clouds like paint half-mixed on a light blue palette:
I try to let the colors bleed into my skin, in hopes I will remember them still
when the leaves are gone and the sun is further.

ii

now that it's september, the green of the trees is
browning at the edges, getting tired (like me. oh, me).
the beauty of decay and the smell of
exhausted anxious life preparing for sleep long
or sleep endless, both of which winter bring.

the grind never stops but it slows
with the advent of winter and the coming of
snowtime stillness stagnancy,
the cold sky flaking apart to drift down to earth
in a near imperceptible slightly offbeat waltz.
predatorless prey animal fast hearts slowing
under the semipermafrost and waiting for the germination
of spring which comes in the wake of unseen shadows.

iii

sky clear in the aftermath of a rainy day, like
the face of a freshly cried child; I am sunk as always
into an implacable depression since my barometric bloodstream
drops inevitable as gravity with the moisture and fog
wrung from the bespectacled eyes of god to fall
down on the streets below.

red lights stretching southward into infinity,
astigmatism-blurry through the still-rain-streaked glass.
it's too humidcold here and I haven't been warm in
months, daily dragging myself unrested out of my
amorphous nightmares, restless and wanting so badly
to sleep. if only I weren't so plagued by this dread
so exhausting I couldn't sleep if I tried.

I know that winter will end,
that the sun will rise.
that the snows will melt back into the earth
to feed the waking trees and flowers and grasses.
something about the sight of the new green on the ends of tree branches
growing by the day always resonates like birdsong in my veins.
and yet, and yet, and yet

I've already forgotten.

iv

every winter I spiral
waiting for spring to let me reset. sometimes
the fog gets so bad I can't tell what language
people are speaking to me in. paranoia follows me wherever I go,
jabbing at me with sharp nails and bony fingers. there are
more days than not where I wake up knowing
that perhaps this day was not one worth getting up for,
that I'll have to struggle to not let the emptiness swallow me
whole (a sisyphean endeavor I'll never be free of
and I'm so fucking tired I could scream).

I haven't been sleeping well lately. by lately,
I mean in the past decade or so. I wake every three hours
to the sound of my nerves clashing and struggle exhaustedly to sink
back into the clutches of unconsciousness.
(I don't *want* to die, but I wouldn't mind

if all of this would just stop.) I want a fucking break. I want to
be able to set down this boulder without it tumbling
down the slope again and dragging me down with it,
back to square one. rock bottom. I can never just stop.
(it's not fucking fair, not even just in an
"I don't deserve to suffer like this" kind of way, but also
in the sense that you'd think that any force exerted
would produce an equal and opposite reaction.
but this particular boulder doesn't obey physics or logic.)

I'm trying so fucking hard to just
be a fucking person, to just carry the infinite weight
of living with myself and in myself and as myself. and I suppose
that's worth something in itself, but it clearly isn't enough.
(it'd be easier to give up, to let the boulder fall
to rock bottom and stay there. to not bother even trying anymore.)

but then I pull in a breath
and remind myself that change is the world is change,
that the sun will rise and the snows will melt and the banks of fog
will someday give way to clear skies (someday,
if not today. nothing is forever is nothing).
shaking my head to clear it, to let centripetal force attempt
chasing away the shadows, wishing my implacable unhappiness
would retreat with the night as the day's primordial frost does
in shyly giving way to the advances of the sun.

urbanite

a city I love that loves me: too much, too much

I spend long stretches of the winter's bleakness wandering the city alone. lonely, but not as a cloud. the clouds here are hegemonic beasts that swallow the distant sun as it strains to make itself heard over the sounds of the city. wearing out my boots little by little as I step daily over salt-sodden slush puddles and soot-snow chimeras. tonight the evening sky spread thin over these miles of island segmented into neat, southwardly-devolving portions is lit primarily by the omnipresent light pollution. the cheshire cat smile of a moon flickers between the solicitous fingers of the barren trees. something about their barrenness speaks to me in a whisper. the moon smiles. the city smiles. I force myself to look away.

I walk through the park, where rhododendrons, folding inwards to make way for their nighttime selves, are separated by wrought iron fences from the homeless people on the benches. in the daytime there is a farmer's market here, with hipster-types hawking organic, locally sourced, slightly-too expensive produce to equally hipster-ish patrons. the homeless people stay out of their way; the clientele of the farmer's market cannot feel good about their ethically superior purchases with them around. merchant and customer alike look away from these reminders of the failures of capitalism, as they are wont to do. they move on. the denizens of this city are well-versed in the art of looking away.

one of the best things about this place is that if someone sees you crying in public, they will ignore you. one of the worst things about this place is that if someone sees you crying in public, they will ignore you. they will avert their gaze. they will try not to noticeably hurry as they walk past you while avoiding eye contact. they will go on with their day, and you, drowning in yourself in the middle of the sidewalk or the subway car or the jogging path along the east river, will just be a mildly unpleasant blip in the course of it. they move on. the denizens of this city are well-versed in the art of looking away.

as always, I find myself standing at the bank of the east river as the winter day hurtles forward into nightfall. contemplating the pros and cons of filling my pockets with stones and throwing myself into the freezing water. I would say I don't know why I always end up here, but that would be a lie.

meanwhile the world goes on, parting around me: red stitches of innumerable taillights winking in and out of existence under the gridlocked clouds, pedestrians picking their ways across the perilous sidewalks overrun by possibly toxic slush. the city is smiling, her arterial streets thrumming with energy and history and secrets and the human germ, and she beckons to me. she calls and my very atoms stir. I cannot look away.

this city, beautiful in a way nothing else can touch, calls me and I have to resist answering. I know what she wants: she wants to be my muse. my only muse. to hold me here forever so that I might immortalize her, worship her, give my soul over to her. go mad over her. she wants me to map out her every inch in words, to sketch out every expression of her ever-changing face. she wants me to set my heart gloriously ablaze, to reduce myself to naught but ash. she wants to eat me alive. she is driving me insane. she is going to kill me. I wish I could look away.

meanwhile the world goes on. it parts around me, the stone in the path of the river. the stone being worn down by the river. the stone being carried forward by the river. this city, my city (and I hers), pulls on my hand, dragging my unwilling steps forward. I am so tired, but I cannot look away. I cannot move on. she is driving me mad. I take a step closer to the water. there is nowhere else to go. she is all there is. I take another step closer to the water. she wants me to die for her, with her, in her. I take another step closer to the water. there is nowhere else to go.

this city, her love is conditional. fickle. she demands and demands and demands from me and I give and I give and I give and it is never enough. she is not content with only a part of me. she is not content, and that makes her aloof. especially in the winter. she's cold to the point of freezing and wants me to do something about it, yet she pulls away from my touch. she won't let me touch her, but she still devours my half-frozen tears before they can fall from my face. it hurts. it hurts, and I love her still. cold and forbidding and beautiful in a way nothing else can touch. she smiles. she calls. what can I do but answer? I take another step closer to the water.

standing at the railing, looking down at the reflections of the light from the bridge, I ask once more what she wants from me. she just laughs. I want to ask her, *are you sure?* but of course she is. so long as I am myself, I am separate from her. she is not content. so long as I am alive. the stone carried forward towards the river. the stone worn down to sand by the river. the sand scattered into the depths of the river, subsumed within its mystery.

meanwhile the world goes on.

the golden mountain

金陵 *(jīnlíng): Literally, "the golden mountain." Pre-Han dynasty name for (and current epithet of) Nanjing, the capital of China's Jiangsu province. The city was the capital city for a number of dynasties, kingdoms, and republican governments (including the Republic of China, which now resides in Taiwan) dating from the third century to 1949.*

i

my first glimpse of nanjing is
this rain-slick runway
with lights shivering in air thirty degrees
cooler than the last city I was in.
below, air traffic controllers, insignificant
beside the behemoths of the sky
they direct, waving us into the terminal.

first impressions aren't everything,
and of course I know that
not everything is about me, but
I can't help but wonder if the rains
followed me here, these gray skies
weighing heavy on my aching bones
but so much a part of me that I could not
leave them behind.

first impressions aren't everything, but
they are lasting ones, the rains
dragging their muddy feet
from winter into spring, but
changing temperament as they do
from distant and hazy to unpredictably violent.

and I wonder if it's because
the depressive fog I packed in
my checked luggage to bring here with me
has given way to what is at best, anxiety,

and at worst, unjust anger:
my father's ghost, haunting me, uncaring
of the leaden blue, ash white, pastel yellow
sky, pressing in close to whisper sweet
nothings which stir through my hair;
or of the fact that the horizons only expand
the further away from home I go.

ii

here is the fish man, wheeling the bike
loaded with his wares,
baskets of water just barely
keeping the slick bodies submerged.
some already in the rictus of death
and others still fighting against it. gasping.

it is spring on the golden mountain,
the crinkled confetti paper of flowers
climbing trellises in colors narcissistic and gaudy.
I try to concentrate on the flowers,
living and breathing in the morning sun,
but I am thinking of the fish.

shaking my head to clear it,
I walk past the monolithic imposition
of some government building or other:
impassive as a mountain, watching over
the clouds of my cigarette smoke
leaving a trail of footprints down the sidewalk
as I make my way past the laborer performing the sisyphean task
of cleaning the filthy streets.

I am on the way to class, but
I am still thinking of the fish. they are dying or dead,
yet here is the velvet softness of new green
which only young leaves in spring possess.
shy as a lover on the first night,
giving to the touch. lovely.

but I suppose, even young as they are,
they are dying too.
and even here, under the lovely cerulean vault
of cumulus-ridden heaven,
I am thinking of how I am dying too.

of how easy it would be to forget
to look both ways. jaywalking is
written into the blood and bones of new yorkers,
but I forget sometimes that most people are afraid to die.
I take a leisurely drag from my cigarette,
my slow suicide clearing the fog in my mind.

I am dying. the leaves and flowers and fish are dying.
either killing ourselves or getting killed.
it is a lovely spring day.

iii

nanjing is a city which was old before new york was even
the faintest hint of an idea in the minds of
white men with names that have too many vowels in a row.
nanjing: the golden mountain, the city of kings. or at least, it was.

now it's a second-rate city by china's own reckoning.
or a 1.5-rate city, if you're professor chen.
older guy, very educated.
nanjing accent so thick he almost sounded taiwanese,
the roundness of his consonants alleviating my homesickness.
the funny kind of patriot that is very proud of being chinese
while also actually criticizing the chinese communist party.

for example, he theorized that the CCP
deliberately quashed the development
of the city which had once been the seat of emperors
and of the republic of china.
mao made the great march north and
did not look back. no pillars of salt here.

chen talked about "first-rate" cities like beijing and shenzhen
with such derision.
upstarts. usurpers. filthy. can't afford anything there.
our food is better, our people are nicer. etcetera.
he seemed very determined to win
the one-sided pissing contest he'd started.

and it was how china seemed to talk about itself.

there was this movie the company I interned at

(publishing house. the office full of party members.

as most publishers in china are) was given tickets to see:

我和我的祖国. *my people, my country*. a propaganda film, essentially.

made for the PRC's seventieth anniversary.

I don't know how to describe it as anything other than

the CCP jerking itself off in public, and then

congratulating itself after achieving a mediocre orgasm.

iv

asian masculinity is a funny thing.
honestly, not much different from
most other kinds of toxic masculinity.
the othering of women.
a view of all emotion as weakness,
aside from anger.
tears the weakest emotion of all.
except when shed in the throes of nationalistic pride.
then it's okay. otherwise,

tears is emotion is womanhood is weakness.
womanhood bound to the home,
bound of the foot.
bound to be married off to another family.
raising a woman-child is like raising
a new year pig. when the time comes,
all the time and energy and food you put into
this creature just goes into someone else's belly,
someone else's family.

the character radical for the word 奴, *slave,* is woman.
女. a woman kneeling.
once the slave is sold,
you don't own it anymore. so what use is it to you?
why waste your love on a pig?

sons, on the other hand.

they carry the yoke of the family name
on their shoulders, dragging the weight
of tradition and filial expectation and
the fate of the nation through the fertile fields.
they plant their seed and if all goes well,
more sons are borne to bear
the same weight onward, upward, forward.
there is no room for womanish weakness.
the weight needs a bearer,
and the only thing a woman should bear is sons.

a woman should never raise her voice in anger.
a woman has no need for anger.
it's not ladylike, I was always told.
keep it to yourself.

as a woman, it is known that
there is no way my anger is my own.
women are not angry like this.
so it must be my father's doing.
his ghost haunting me. possessing me.
the wrath of the first son who can do no wrong.
mama's special boy.

III

*"Let me but gaze on what I may not touch
And feed the aching fever in my heart."*

- OVID, METAMORPHOSES (TRANSLATED
BY A.D. MELVILLE)

the republic of heaven

they say our universe is just one of many, infinitely many
splitting off at every variation, down to the subatomic.
and when god closes a door,
that door opens in another universe.
like ours. unlike ours.

somewhere out there, there's another us
older than we were here but still together.
like us. unlike us. there, you might see
me half asleep, filled to the seams with
the sound of your hand in mine and
our footprints trailing backwards.
the other me wouldn't feel so sad anymore, even if
the gods were laughing as we burned
under their magnifying glasses and the sun.

here, where we are (where are you now?)
we were just children in the garden
of all things good and evil.
god told me that if I loved you
I would surely die from the inside out
but I couldn't stand being alone
with the sound of my own voice so I
fell from heaven to you
and I forgot about the difference.
so imagine my shock at the pain the shame the cold.
at your anger. at my scars.

on the other hand, in this other place,
this other time, this other possibility,
the me there is still naive enough to think
that death is for other people.
not for us. and certainly not for you.
I swore I'd fistfight with death themselves, the bastard,
if they dared lay a finger on you
and you just laughed. said you liked my spunk.
my willingness to bloody my hands in ichor
for the sake of making you mine.

not every version of you loves this about me though.
not every version of you loves me.
not every version of you loves me anymore.
some versions might not have even met
some version of me. our lives might never have
intersected, might have never been passerby
in close enough proximity to the right time and place
to make it work. not every version of us can make it work.

here, where we are,
if the angels sang in reverse
for long enough to wander back in time to you and me,
you would laugh and say you loved me
and in reverse it might not even sound bitter
as tears drain back into your eyes.

the singing would continue
and birds would fly backwards towards the north
as we walked backwards hand in hand,
getting younger in the streets we'd grown up in,
the snow scattering into the skies,
gravity dragging the moon backwards through its phases.

o, the joy of it all.
airplanes would fly out of
the frozen river and screams would
be swallowed into the passengers' mouths
as geese materialized from the engines
and then reformed into a backwards v
to head inexorably south.

the angels, still singing, would watch as
you take my hand and my apologies
crawl back under my skin.
they would watch and maybe smile
(a little bitterly if the divine are kind),
the strains of their song slowly coming to an end.
the end. our end. as the echoes faded,
you would laugh and say you loved me.

sucker punch

i

I dreamed of you again last night.
the unbearable and inevitable human urge
to prostrate oneself before another
compels me like always to call you. but
no. you don't want to hear it.
and you don't want to love me anymore.
(your voice a constant echo:
god, what did I do to deserve this?)
I think. so I ignore it. like always.

my therapist says I need to trust people more.
be more vulnerable. make connections.
I always think of you suppressing a smile,
biting back the words *I told you so.*
I haven't thrown myself into the hudson yet
because of my tethers to the living.
and also because of the pollution.
but mostly because of my connections,
tethering me to this side of the river.

but god. being vulnerable with others is just.
so fucking hard. impossibly hard.
"taking the SAT naked and your teeth falling out
all over your answer sheet"-nightmare material.
should I (a) put my frightened little sparrow of a heart
in your hands and submit myself to the mortifying ordeal
of being known by another? or should I just
(b) pretend I'm alright with waking up alone

now into forever in the silence eternal,
until my restless soul can finally fizzle out into nothingness
and my body can feed the trees?
mark your answers on the scantron, please.

and besides, even if you didn't take the opportunity of
my vulnerability to crush my sparrow-heart
into a pulp of bloody feathers, it wouldn't matter.
inexplicable, self-destructive madness is my forte.

I tell myself that when you insist I'm not a burden,
it's a lie. when you tell me you love me,
it's just because you're afraid that you're my only
tether to the living. that you actually hate me,
but the connection is made and you're too kind
to cut me off. to let me die.

or maybe it isn't that inexplicable.
self-destructive, mad, yes.
but not inexplicable. it's as simple as this:
I couldn't stand the thought of losing you,
so I pushed you away
(*what did I do to deserve this?*)

ii

all these years, so many people and things
have come and gone. but not my sadness.
(*what did I do to deserve this?*)
the most familiar of suffocating embraces.
the most comforting torture.
my oldest friend. my magnetic north.
my baseline. I'm so at home here at rock bottom
that you making me happy is terrifying.

you don't deserve this.
and I don't deserve you:
you're better off without me,
without the dead weight of my despair
sleeping in the space between us at night.
I think. I'm pretty sure.

but anyway, no matter what,
I can always count on the sadness.
sinking its claws into me.
me clinging back just as tight.
tethering me here. rock bottom.

iii

[once, early on]
you turned to me in bed.
eyes and body and voice soft with wonder
and contented sleepiness. a murmur of
god, what did I do to deserve this?
paired with a smile blurring the edges of your face.

[sometime in the middle, when the unraveling begins.
my tongue tied in a cherry stem of a knot.]
a thousand sentences conceived and aborted in my mouth:
there's mercury in my veins;
when the temperature falls, so does my mood.
or: *sometimes I feel raw, overstimulated;*
everything runs over my bare nerve endings instead of my skin
and it burns.
or perhaps: *april showers bring may flowers,*
but march showers just bring me down.

or maybe: *my roommate doesn't say anything anymore*
when I spend a quarter of an hour wandering around the apartment,
looking for something I can't put a name to.
or: *there's this awful hollow ache*
where my heart should be (where is it now?)
that the hypochondriac in me worries is a heart attack
but the suicidal poet in me embraces.

but it's no use. you could never understand.

it doesn't rain like this in LA.

you could never understand.

[later on, towards the end:

a cross-country phone call.

your voice mere imagination. blurred by distance.

warped by anger. a gauntlet thrown,

the vehemence familiar by now.]

god, what did I do to deserve this?

[I swallow around the clog of despair in my throat,

muster up anger. pretend I cannot smell

the edge of longing desperation in your voice.]

modern love

nowadays I love you like
"is this love or lust?"
like waiting hours for your name
to come up on my screen.
like I'll be your manic pixie dream girl
or your sugar baby
or whoever you want me to be
just so long as you want me.

I love you like
having no sense of moderation and
listening to your favorite song
over and over and over and over and over again
until you can't stand it anymore.

I love you like
you only pay attention to me when you're single
so I burn when you aren't,
like the smell of your cologne on someone else
drives me insane,
like I don't know anything
about your new girl except that
she won't love you like I do
and you might not want her to.

this modern love:
it eats me alive
and coughs me up on your doorstep
battered and bruised,
but I love you like

I'll beg to be let in
so I can tangle my fingers in your hair,
lick my way into your mouth,
and crawl under your skin.

I love you like
the sound of your voice makes
my body ring like a tuning fork,
like every night I dream of you and
I wake up every morning
with my skin aching,
the memory of your dream-hands on me
haunting me into my waking hours.

I love you like I am
obsessed
to the point that I am always
painfully, thoroughly aware
when you are inches or feet or miles away,
every nerve ending I have
constantly straining towards you.

this modern love:
it makes me itch like an addict.
makes me capable of anything.
and it doesn't matter if you don't feel the same about me, baby,
because the heart wants what the heart wants and
baby, I'll die for you.
I'll kill for you.
I'll do anything for you but
leave you alone.

the garden

a progression, or a degradation. there is no difference.

i

in my filthy mouth I hold an apple and
you take the rotting thing from me so that
god will cast us into the dirt (innocence dejected
in a snow-white bed: am I the tempter, the tempted,
or the apple itself?)

ii

the surface of a seemingly placid lake, yet
the leaves still drifting softly to
the other side (where is the current that carries them?
where are you now? and who are you with?). with you,
I am never jealous;
there is no cause. with you,
my spring of jealousy never runs dry.

iii

in this little corner of campus there is
the reverent semi-quiet presided over
by the trees shushing noisy offenders.
the days until I see you again outnumbering even
the flower petals dropping slowly
from pregnant branches to float down
to the ground, passing
slowly, but inevitably: these days
until once again I can be more to you than
a pretty face and some pretty words.

the miles between us dwarfing
every leaf on every tree here, but
know that my love for you will outlast them all
like this cool stone of a pagoda,
crouching quiet in the wood, with
seats wide enough for two.

iv

the rain drains into the sky and I swallow the sound of your name.
the sun switches off behind the curtains of clouds.
if we could go back, if only;
(the cherry blossoms of your smile blooming)
I'd bite my tongue and drown on my blood and
let it be instead of begging for you to love me.
you were just the first rain in months on a land cracked by drought
and I was the fool who thought it would last.

V

actions speak louder than words,
but the sound of your love is
a song I can't quite remember anymore.
but it's alright; I'd be alright
with forgetting your voice if I could still project
fantasies onto the projector screen of your skin
(a canvas of living bronze: rodin's adam
(the first of man, and I your first) come to life)

vi

adam and eve walk out of the eastern gate
and a flaming sword divides them.
what they birth is good and bad,
but then cain smites his brother and there is only
the bad.
and how can you even look each other in the eye afterwards,
knowing that together, you created a monster
which killed your joy and cursed you?

so there are two possible stories from here on out:
the garden of eden wilting in the absence of its caretakers.
the animals going nameless, the grass going dry,
the lion eating the hawk eating the rat eating the plants.
the plants learning thorns, the fruit learning poison,
(the first of your women should have been better)
because why love when you can fuck,
why play when you can fight?

or: the garden growing wild.
overgrown, overtaking.
becoming unrecognizable.
(exes are exes for a reason:
if paradise were to be regained
it would be with god's grace
given to someone not banned from
the parts of you now unknown to my eyes)

花心

花心 huāxīn: (adj.) fickle in love, unfaithful. Literally, "flower-hearted."

darling, you ought to stay away from me
because I'm that bitch, that slut, that cunt
they should've warned you about.
it's not that I'll not love you: of course (I think) I will
(I do/do I) but my heart is sakura at even the best of times,
all the permanence of shifting sand and

it's only a matter of time before
I pick at the seams of youmeus because I'm bored
or I'm restless or I'm tired or I wish I was
elsewhere elsewho elsewhat
or because the despair constantly crawling up
my throat like nausea has become
too loud to ignore and I'm too busy
trying to blink away the autophagic anguish
welling up behind my eyes to pay you any mind.

it's just borderline
personality/insanity/instability/insatiability/insecurity
in love to hate to everything in between
and beyond; it's not your fault/it's not my fault/
it's both our faults/it's nobody's fault/it's
my fault/it's my personality/my
problem/my mine mine

mine/I want you to be mine until you are
and then I want to consume and be consumed by you.
I want to be the rain caressing
the planes of your face and
filling your lungs; I want to be the scorched earth
campaign of your love life, sherman razing a path to the sea
and leaving footprints in your ash.
after we make love/war/
mistakes (yours or mine?) I want you
to swear your heart to me

and then I want nothing to do with you, since
I am the general and the army and the sea,
flanking you on all sides so I might
devour your tears and make them mine.
I want you to break yourself on the shore of my blood
and run out with the tide, with the end,
with the shreds of my sanity clutched in your fist.
I'll love you and a thousand others all at once
and I'll never be happy
with any of you because you're just not enough
and it's not your fault; all things change
and end and die and youmewe aream no exception

purgatory

i

a man made of fire smiles and asks what I'm thinking,
and all I can manage to say is *I have always been both
a pyromaniac and a masochist.*

it's all cyclical, inexorable:
I bleed I floss I bleed.
I wake I cry I dream again.
I bleed you weep I bleed.
I kiss I tell you weep.
I tell him I love him but what I really mean to say is that

he is the latest in a long list of projective vessels.
I mean to say *I am not content with your mere
hands in the thicket of my hair or your love;
I want your bleeding heart in my mouth
and your blood flooding my lungs;
I want you burned down to ash so I can breathe you in
in all your carcinogenic glory;
I want you to build a pyre of my bones
and throw yourself upon it;
I want unambiguity to reign and
you to be its subject its abject its aspect;
I mean tell me how you love me
so I can learn how to make you cry;
or tell me what you're afraid of
so I can devour you instead;*

or I mean that *if you tell me you love me*
someday I'll learn to hate you too;
or that *no matter how I try, everything I've ever made is*
self portraiture, even when it's your body sprawled on these sheets
of paper, rendering my thoughts and inhibitions naught but ash;
even and especially when I tell you
I love you; cycling and spinning and
returning to me myself and I/I wish I loved you/
I wish I knew you/I wish you could be more

to me. I'm sorry, for whatever that's worth
that all I can ever make of you is selective repetition.
alas (alas), I run from you
back to me, so that I might die by my own hand and not yours
I am (not yours) sorry. really.

ii

a man made of fire asks why I keep writing about him
and I say *you know when you write or say or read a word*
over and over and over until it loses all meaning?
(if I were more of a romantic, I'd say I wrote about him
so he could live forever but that would be a lie I am
far more in love with the him I've written than I am with him,
and it's what I've written into existence that I hope outlives us both)

still, I think I do want him. or maybe I just want him to try
and fill this empty space in my chest cavity, singing with echoes
or to try and hold my hands and keep me from dissolving
into the rain. *you deserve better, though*, I might say
if I was a better person, if I could extricate myself
from the clutches of that greedy-toothed beast of a sleeping dragon
lurking just below the surface of the storm-tossed waters of my mind

iii

a woman made of fire asks me if I want something
different from her than I do from everyone else and the answer is
of course not, who do you think I am? (do you know?
do I?) so it doesn't matter who
you are; only what I can make you, who how when where I can

write you; but I am at least sweeter with her (the constellations
of her freckles, of her eyes, make anything else impossible):
she asks me what I dream about and I bite down on my tongue to drown out
the words *you, actually*, but I think she hears them anyway,
(I have dreamed of you so/too often of late)
if the smile flitting like candlelight between her eyes and
her mouth is anything to go by.
instead I say *tell me no lies and I'll tell you my truth; the sun rises only
when it wants to match your windblown eyes.*

I say *the huntress' bow of your smile,*

the most elusive of artemisial metaphors

shyly emerging from a peach-pink-tinged sky, sometimes makes me want to cry.

because saccharine as it is, it's better than saying *I keep having this dream lately*

where we're at brunch with a group of others and sitting too close.

you have your arm around me and you keep

pressing kisses into my hair to punctuate

your sentences, and I want it so badly I wake up hardly able to speak

because the thought of you is burning its way up my throat.

better than saying *I want you/things so badly but I never ask*

because you can never match up

to the hazy outlines of my poems/of my dreams, colored with their easy affection.

iv

I know not anything beyond myself above myself below outside inside myself;
all else cannot be but echoes, shadows of shadows

on the walls of the cave. I know you not and I love you I love you,
I love the blurred shadow of the reflection of the idea of you, warped
through the lens of my gaze. you are beyond the reaches

of what my exhausted mind can render, and yet
you are but a figment of my imagination, a mere passing thought I love
you I love me I love me not I know myself not I am

still trying to free myself from the clutches of
this sleeping dragon without waking it,
but there is that constant inertial exhaustive lingering feeling
of *perhaps I should could would just stay here, clinging to the shadows
chained around my wrists and ankles.*
of *perhaps I could stop fighting the tide, stop fighting with fire.*
of *perhaps I could let gravity make a lover of me. of me, the fighter.*
I'm so tired, anyway. too tired to keep afloat.
perhaps I should drown.

the insomniac, longing

the hands of sleep disheveling my hair:
a cruel lover she is, always leaving me
aching, unsatisfied. always
making me presents of bruised eyes and cracking joints.
leaving me. wanting more.
simultaneously pushing me away and
rendering my extrication from her clutches
an impossibility. the memory of her
whispers to me when I am away. drawing me in.
keeping me out. at night I lie awake,
listening to the cicada-humming of my tinnitus,
missing her.

time passes differently at night as I remember.
it wasn't always this with her. once, it was:
streetlight blanketing the visage of midnight like snowfall.
the sky undone and her under it,
precipitous and lovely against the backdrop of
the cracked sidewalk. my thoughts weaving
nonsensically. mere association in place of actual coherence.
I love you. I love you not. how could I ever not love you?
I love you. I love you not. the weight of expectation
like a scarf knotted just a tad too tight.
a gentle constriction. but warm. the warmth coming
from me. but at least it holds it for me.
I love you. I love you. I swear it. I love you.

I am so full of words that I cannot speak,
full as the sky and its stars scattered across
that lovely dark expanse. we are so far apart
and forever growing further. growing farther.
growing emptier. losing order.

that is the nature of entropy. but I love her,
because how could I not, because I love her,
because last night in my brief fitful wakeful dream she said
she loved me. she said she loved me,
so why won't she take me home?
I'm so tired. please take me home. she said
she loved me. why won't she let me go home?
no matter how close I walk,
it pulls away. no matter how I run to keep up,
to catch her, she pulls away.
she pulls me away. pulls me apart.

she won't let me go, won't let me leave
(*and why would I leave her?*
I love her.) but I guess it doesn't matter.
because some of the time

some of the time it's good.
it's divine; she's divine
and I dissolving into her.
dissolving until I am no longer myself.
I am no longer able to tear myself away from her
without causing irrevocable damage;
the pulse of my heart whispering *I love you love you* ~~*love you not*~~ *I'm not*
worried I love you I love you ~~*and you love me not*~~

and it doesn't matter if it hurts (when it's good it's divine

so it's alright if the good only comes once in a while).

I take the bruises, the lonely nights, the worried glances of my friends

in stride, made easier by the fact that I see them

less and less. I have no energy for anything or anyone else.

she is all there is and I have nothing

but love for her.

mid autumn

中秋節 *(zhōngqiūjié): (n.) the Mid-Autumn Festival. Like Thanksgiving,*
a harvest time festival to be spent with one's family.

there is no man lonelier
than the poets of my people
spending this time of year watching
the moon, lamenting that
as achingly distant as
that virgin temptress may be,
the ones they long most for
are even further.

a moon pockmarked by a crater.
a circular table broken by an empty seat.

IV

"Not knowing what he sees, he adores the sight;
That false face fools and fuels his delight.
You simple boy, why strive in vain to catch
A fleeting image? What you see is nowhere;
And what you love—but turn away—you lose!
You see a phantom of a mirrored shape;
Nothing itself; with you it came and stays:
With you it too will go, if you can go!"

- OVID, METAMORPHOSES (TRANSLATED
BY A.D. MELVILLE)

"if you're reading this, i'm gone."

from a suicide note, scheduled and shared posthumously.

every media a social thing,
contextualized and brought to fruition
by the interplay between the text and the consumer.
consumption, digestion, excretion. repeat.

but this. this is something else.
this is a space on a screen which at best is rife with
anthemic declarative indubitables wrought in blue light
and more than a hint of curation. at worst it is a cesspool a
whirlpool a quagmire a vessel of performative pain a bubble of
quicksand. a hundred million voices at once screaming *I am
the main character I am I am I am a Janusian conundrum I am
the gaoler and the prisoner I am the hangman's collection of boots
I am the spark and the tinder and the flame and the ash
I am I am I am I am HERE please see me hear me love me hate me
SEE ME as I am as I am not as I want to be seen
I want to be SEEN please please please—*

how lovely the madness. all these faceless rootless voices.
arguing loving hating debating lying confessing sharing celebrating
teaching learning mourning growing showing
maddening. living. dying.
eternal ephemeral atonal screeching echoing in the void.
how lovely the madness. constant. and all gone in a moment.

and I am torn, because how radical the act of kindness is
in spaces such as these,
because how kind of me to act as the warden of my shallow-built anger:
shadows swallowed smothered smiled nothing wrong and all is well
though you are wrong and my bones turn to ash
in the face of my wildfire wrath tamped down to embers but never put out
I can never put it out (do I want to

put it out? I wish sometimes I could be/do
more than/this/me that has never learned
to bloody her knuckles her teeth her knees/give
in to the part of me that burns
olympian fire angry waiting simmering wishing I could be
deadly edge and killing blow)

but then again.
there is that other part of me which is closer to wherever
the heart of the mind of the root of my soul is.
that wishes the world would be kinder to our fragile sapient carapaces.
that is the caged bird singing that is the song that is the sky.

I wish I could look away from the ongoing landslide
but the unfortunate human tendency towards morbid fascination with
so-called degeneracy makes hypocrites of us all (look away/I dare you).
I wish I could resist the urge to add my voice to the cacophony.
to *leave my last mark on this world.*

we live in echo chambers of our own making because we are just so
in love with our own voices and yet
we don't seem to say much,

listening only for space to respond
/making our own spaces(/voids/spaces)
to pedestal to pedant to
perform to perchance
to dream to sleep to w/make
infinities of spaces
infinities of
nothing/of
potential

sicarius

i

judas, the death in your kiss inexorable inevitable ineffable, you are
the death of me and the savior of man. you are the catalyst of the end
of the beginning of the end of all things.

judas, my friend, no man is an island but you (kiss and tell;
sailing to a new land to run from your persecution your guilt.
the island of the mind:
will you ever be able to leave?).
tell me, is this how you treat all your friends?

judas, or jack, or whatever your name is:
the little blond-haired god is dead, pulled to bloody shreds
in the low tide of blissless dionysian ecstasy on the beach
of the island of the mind (of the devil with the flies in his mouth;
conch shattered. my poor dear simon undone.)

judas, my child:
my poor fool is hanged.
it is not your fault, jack my dear;
you are only the catalyst.
but will you ever be able to leave?

ii

[island, exterior. the flies have been biting my face.]
judas, my dear, let's play simon says. I'm ~~a fool~~ simon,
and you are the maenads. I mean children. I mean men.
[you are dancing in circles, chanting of
the beast. speak of the devil.]

simon says I see you there dancing and I wanted to tell you
about the things I saw, the devil I spoke to.
[you are dancing in circles and gnashing your teeth]

there's nothing to be afraid of,
there is no beast. ~~what are you doing?~~
[the overwhelming sounds of teeth and claws
and teeth and claws and
simon, me, drowning]
~~simon says please listen to me~~

~~you're hurting me please~~
[teeth and claws, teeth and claws]
~~simon says please there is nothing to fear~~
~~you have nothing to fear from me~~
[teeth/claws/teeth/claws/hands/blood]
~~please stop hurting me please please stop~~
(did the son of god pray while hanging from the cross?)
[you howling over the sounds of my bloodied voice and
the making of a bacchanal offering]

iii

judas iscariot, the island you are/the island that is
not an island/that is a nation/that is
a country raised on a diet of blood,
built on a mountain of corpses.

whose? mine, of course (kiss me, my friend:
gifts of smallpox blankets, trails of tears.
land of the free. for whom?).
you don't belong here either.
where are you from really?

I don't know if it really matters
whether I am killed by your hands
or your words or your kiss
or by someone else's hands
or on a cross I am nailed to
or watched over by a priest
or hanging from your rope
or at the hands of the police
or under the whip
or after I bear the spawn of the white devil.
what matters (in my biased opinion)
is that I am dead.
I am dead. and it is your fault.

you/your nation/your destruction/your darling/your babe:
you whet its appetite young and it has never stopped glutting
since. you should know the author never dies, not really.
in the sense of legacy yes but there's no
truly divorcing a product from its progenitor, because (especially
when it comes to art) so much of it is so self-reflective. self-reflexive.
congratulations, my friend,
on finding the key to immortality.

so, lady liberty, let us rebuild
these teeming shores, where the
homeless, tempest-tost, huddled masses (wretched
refuse) yearning to breathe free are running rampant.

iv

iscariot, my friend, you die in one of two ways:
you walk into a field and shake hands with your guilt and then
trip, overcome by the smell of the blood on your hands.
falling headlong, bursting asunder, entrails feeding the earth you bought
with your blood money (not your blood to give:
what was that thirty silver worth?)

or: ~~the son of god~~ the man you kissed said that all those who take the sword
will perish by the sword, but your sword has not
left its place; your sword is your word is your kiss is your hand,
and it is by your hand you perish, breathless and dancing.

either way it ends the same: the land your money ~~(not your blood
to give)~~ bought is become a potter's field, a field of blood.
a place to bury strangers.
either way, it always ends the same.
inevitable and ineffable.

and you, my dear?
burn.

---

*Note: The word "sicarius," which Judas's surname is likely etymologically
derived from, is Latin for "assassin" or "murderer."*

fallen

the blamed women: the box, the apple.
gifts within curses within gifts and all
their flaws. their birthrights. their charms.
they were just so *young*,
the first of women (made of clay, made of man)
with no one before them to tell them

you are but children of the world, the first
of our kind. and have known nothing and knew nothing
and now are nothing but your devastation your wake.
the world before placid, with gods walking among men.
but not among you. you were made distant.
beautiful and curious and loving. but distant.
your only tether to the gods a man who loves you.
a man who you were made for.
the man. one and only. you had no other choice.

little one, you need not yet know
what it is to preface the bearing of the burden of life
(your hips have not widened your breasts are not full)
this is not your burden to bear;

who put this weight on your shoulders?
the weight of your life and new life and our life and old,
of the survival of the roots of mankind,
of the spoils of war, of the wreckage of gods.

the opening of the box. the fall from grace.
the only things left to you in the aftermath
your man (*the* man), your pain, and
hard-won hope.

so few see the road laid *before* your disaster
that we your daughters, your sisters, we now
bear your burden your legacy your body your blame.
the evils of mankind released. we cast from paradise.
o, woe is man. woe is me.
(far greater the woe is woman.)

but consider the gun pointed at a head.
who do we blame? the weapon?

隨著

隨著 *suízhe: (v.) to go along with, to comply with.*

the birth of dumplings happens most often within
the sacred circle of women; the work of apparently natural nurture
for which my hands and voice are not nearly soft enough,
the skins tearing as I try to force them
into the right shape, as I pack
too much stuffing into one wrapper.
I am 太貪心, *too greedy*, the women always say,
clicking their tongues in practiced disapproval.

unlike this initiated circle of gentle hands and birthing hips
I am too opinionated, too rough, too angry,
too americanized. 太貪心. I take up more space than I should.
that's not very ladylike. they say I will learn when I am older (and did someone
say that to you, all those years ago, before
time and distance and a man pulled your teeth out?)
that someday I'll find a man and want to settle down,
sign away my father's name, progenate. *someday you'll see.*

the women of my culture are supposed to be
quiet obedient sitstayshutup because
it's just the way things are but
even on the best of days I dance on
the razor's edge between rage
and despair so even though I bite my tongue until I taste blood
I cannot help but ask why Him anyway? God is

an incomprehensible pluralism beyond gender so why
Him Him Him and not me? why should I
sitstayshutup, why must I nurture?
why is my anger wrong? are my atlantean shoulders
not broad enough, man enough, enough enough? do I have
no choice but to be one half
of a heterosexual whole penned in by a white picket fence,
to birth two point five progeny and then till death do us part?
why am I not enough?
why am I
not enough?

I yell until my throat is raw and my voice goes. at that point,
the women can sigh in relief and settle their feathers back over the status quo,
resume the conception and birth and death of dumplings
in peace, because I am finally silent.

the middle kingdom

i

at home, when I walk alone at night, it is with
keys between my fingers. pepper spray in one pocket.
a knife in the other. phone in hand. ready. alert.
but at home what I am afraid of has eyes I can see,
is something I could feasibly fight off with keys or pepper spray
or by calling the right person.

not here. not here.
my hands are empty.
knives require a license.
they are watching.
the corner of that building.
the look in that man's eyes.
spyware-bloated apps.
watching.always.watching.

through the window of the bullet train, the high rail,
I see it. them. a country conspiring
to keep me (an american idiot) in flux between the living and the dead.
holding me down with my head underwater, occasionally letting me

up to gasp for air; they watch me endlessly unblinkingly unfailingly but they
do nothing. I know they know I know them now I know they don't
want my blood on their hands but they are just
watching,always,watching I can feel
their eyes their hands their head shoulders knees and toes

awareness of something~~something~~*something* just over my shoulder
making the hair on my body stand up. a mammal feeling threatened,
hackles raised. ~~it's nothing~~. I know it. I know them. they know me. they are
watching. watching. always.
the woman's eyes follow me.
scanning my ID at the entrance.
the unblinking pupil of a lens.

brother mao, big brother,
brother dearest comrade mine, (they saved you a spot
flooded with formaldehyde to keep you safe)
if you really can walk the line between these capitalistic communistic dreams
then why are you watching me, western dragon-jealous,
hungry ghost-demanding, restless corpse-liminal?

ii

mother country mother mine, you are
the fount from which my bloodline springs.
from which my traditions rise (from which
my anger feeds). is that why
you unblinkingly unbreathingly
think you know what is best for me?
because I am neither dead nor alive? because I belong

nowhere and to no one and to nothing?
because I am both both and half and neither?
(in the truest expression of parenthood,
you made me this way) because my
mother dearest father mine are the product of
an island countryless country
which all the king's horses and all the king's men
could not force back into your womb,
which is the root of the weed which has spread its seeds
from sea to shining sea to the empireless(?) empire?

mother country mother mine,
you made me the way I am.
so did they, my own country
which so often does not see me as its own.
one look at me, and you know
I do not belong to you.
nor do I belong to them.
I am the exile. one foot in, one out.
born into liminality and doomed to it.

to them, it is my face which marks me. *other*.
the slant of my cheekbones, the bridge of my nose.
not to mention the languages twisting my tongue.
the smell of my mother's cooking.
and my name. or to be precise,
my father's name.

to you, it is my anger which marks me. 外國人.
my volume. my refusal to lay down, sit down, shut up.
the fact that when I get drunk,
I start taunting you. tempting you to kill me,
knowing full well that you'd want to.
and my name. my father's name.
marking me as not one of yours,
but of a country(?) bred from your blood.

if you could get away with it,
you'd sew my mouth shut.
if they could get away with it,
they'd sew my eyes shut.
you're more alike than you think, you know.

外國人 *(wàiguórén): foreigner; outsider.*
Note: China's name for itself is 中國 *(zhōngguó).* 中 *translates to "center"*
or "middle." 國 *translates to "nation" or "kingdom."*

fear

i

you're waiting for a train and it's cold. you're alone except for a man down the platform that keeps (not very) surreptitiously looking at you, perhaps deciding whether or not he should make the effort of trying to talk to you. you tuck your hair behind the ear facing him to expose the fact that you're wearing headphones and hope he gets the message. he doesn't. he approaches, and your stomach twists into fetal position and plunges for cover somewhere down by your feet. you can barely hear what he's saying over the roaring in your ears. he keeps trying to demand your attention and you keep giving the shortest, least committal answers you can think of as you repeatedly glance at the clock, watching the viscous minutes until the train comes slowly trickle away.

you're a pretty little thing, he says, and your hand, which is in your coat pocket wrapped around your keys, clenches until the metal threatens to break skin. you've read somewhere that they're actually not a great weapon, since you're just as likely to break all the bones in your hand as you are to actually cause enough damage to discourage a determined assailant, but they're all you have; you're grasping for straws, praying to someone, anyone, that the train will come and it won't be empty and you will get home without this man's steps or eyes or hands or mind following you.

ii

you're at a club with your friends and you're hovering both on the far side of tipsiness and around the edges of the room, nursing the last of your fourth or fifth drink. drunk you has three incarnations: the poet waxing eloquent, the elated flirt, and the furious typhoon bottled up in a shell of a person. the latter is the most common of the three, and you're only here because your friends love the music here and love to dance, and you don't give a fuck about anything but the strength of these drinks, so you're trying your best not to ruin the night even though you're not in the mood for it.

a man offers to buy you a drink (*you're a pretty little thing*) and you smile the least poisonous smile you can manage through gritted teeth as you turn him down, excusing yourself by way of the drink you already have in hand. he gets annoyed and you sidle out towards the bathroom. there, you touch up your bloodred lipstick and take deep breaths, reminding yourself that you are a full six inches shorter and perhaps sixty pounds lighter than that man, so you will lose if it comes to a physical altercation. not to mention it would most certainly ruin your friends' night.

the winds of the typhoon die down enough that you can slam back the rest of your drink and join your friends on the dance floor, where you try to embody as little of your slowly simmering wrath as possible. in the little cluster where you're dancing there's a girl (~~a pretty little thing~~) being felt up by the same man who offered to buy you a drink earlier. you recognize the prey animal look in her eyes and when he's distracted you lean in and ask in the lowest whisper you can manage over the pounding music whether or not she wants you to get her away from him. she nods and you loop in your friends to playfully pull her out of his grasp and barricade her in a happy, spinning circle of dancing femininity.

the hunted edge in her eyes softens, but it doesn't go away, especially because he doesn't seem to have bought that this girl is your friend. he grabs you by the shoulder and roughly pulls you around to face him, demanding to know what the hell your problem is. the typhoon swells beyond all hope of containment, and the shell cracks. you knee him in the groin. as he doubles over in pain, you put a hand on his shoulder and shove him, hard, away from you. he tumbles onto the floor and his friends start shouting. you leave the club alone, telling your friends to go on without you, and walk home with an expression on your face that makes the few passersby skitter out of your way.

iii

you're in a shitty bar downtown with a couple of friends you haven't
seen in a while, but the ones you like better leave early and you're there
with a few that you don't know or like as much. friends of friends, that
sort of thing. one is a guy who's got a long-distance girlfriend that
you've met a few times when she flew over once to spend a week with
him. nice girl. he's a handsy flirt when he's drunk though, and a persistent one too, nice girlfriend be damned. he's got one too-warm hand
on your thigh that he keeps trying to slide higher up, even when you've
told him in no uncertain terms to keep his goddamn hands off you.
you grab his middle finger and pull backwards hard until it's perpen-
dicular to his wrist, and he pulls his hand away.

the vague hope you feel that he might've gotten the message fades
quickly though, because he puts his arm around your shoulders
instead and pulls you up against his side. you pull back an elbow and
drive it into his groin, but he just grins with a half-moaned out *fuck
yeah, harder,* breath reeking of fourloko and soju and the determina-
tion of a horny man. his moist whisper in your ear informs you (~~pretty
little thing~~) that he likes it rough, wants to fuck like animals until
you're both screaming. that he loves it when they put up a fight. you
splash a drink in his face and slide out from under his arm and take off.
when you get home, you lock and deadbolt the door before sprinting
into the bathroom and emptying your stomach until you're gasping.
for the next hour, you sit on the floor leaning against the wall, weeping.

accountability

i

after sandy hook, we had an active shooter drill at school.
we'd had them before, perfunctory as fire drills
or school assemblies. but this one was different. this one was
a collective held breath, hands clenched together,
almost in prayer. this one was the knowledge that
it could be me. it could be me.

this one, when a faculty member in the hallway
tested the locked door handle, his broad silhouette
filling the backlit window set in the door
with its thin shade drawn down,
the whole room of fourteen-year-olds,
sitting curled up around ourselves on the floor
against the wall, flinched as one body at
the sudden rattling of the door.

one of my classmates began to cry,
as silently as possible, her hands
clamped over her mouth
to keep the wordless fear from escaping.
the whole room as one body, with one thought:
it could be me. it could be real.
it could be me.

even on days without drills, I would plan
escape routes, defense tactics.
throw textbooks. the stapler.
that heavy three-hole punch.
desks jammed against the door.
how many people could we fit in the closet?
or under the teacher's desk?
the fall from the window: was it survivable?

ii

adam toledo was only thirteen.
he was thirteen, and now
he can never be anything other than thirteen.
he was thirteen, and now
he's a name demanded to be said,
for justice demanded
and too often indefinitely deferred.

there's so many people that just
look away, explain away. demand to know
where his parents were, why was he out
at two in the morning. and to that I say
it doesn't matter.
it doesn't.
fucking.
matter.

what's it gonna take for you to realize that?
it doesn't fucking *matter*.
it doesn't matter
if you're thirteen or forty-six or *seven*, for christ's sake.
it doesn't matter if you're breaking the law
or not; it doesn't matter if you're armed
or not; it doesn't matter if you're compliant
or not. it doesn't matter
how you identify, what your profession is,
how much money you make;
if you're a mother, a brother, a lover, a friend;
if you play the violin or with toy guns;
if you can't breathe, you can't breathe, you *can't breathe*;

that you're just out jogging or birdwatching or
trying to live your goddamn life.
it doesn't matter if you're awake or asleep,
in your own home or anywhere else.

it doesn't matter. none of it does.
they'll kill you and they'll say it was your fault
and there's no way them kneeling on your goddamn neck
for *nine fucking minutes* was what killed you;
no way them putting you in a chokehold
cutting off blood flow to your brain
and then dosing you ketamine was what killed you.
it was your asthma, your drugs, your heart condition.
your crime. your fault.

they'll kill you and they'll say it was an accident,
that they meant to go for their taser,
that they were having a bad day,
that they thought your skittles or your phone or your sandwich
was a gun. that they were scared.
they'll say they were just
doing their job. protect and serve.

how many children of color are out there right now,
reading adam's name and thinking the same thought:
it could be me?

iii

whenever someone bitches about
kids these days not being respectful
or some asinine shit like that, I always want to say:
look at your hands. look at the filth
that's all over them. look closer.
realize it's blood, drying slowly, thickly.
it's blood, new coats being painted on
before the last has had time to dry.

this is the world you are leaving to us.
your children. your blood.
our blood, on your hands.
your hands which may not have built this world,
but which desperately hold together
the shitshow of an abomination that your predecessors built.
where these kinds of tragedies happen so regularly
that we're growing numb, desensitized.
atrocities normalized as people acclimatize.
what for?
what the hell for?

why does it matter so much to you
that things stay the way that they are?
is this working for you, the bricks of our buildings
mortared together with the slowly congealing blood of your children?
your fucking *children*? human fucking beings
that you brought into this world, dying?
doesn't that matter to you at all?

what are they even dying for?
your right to bear arms? your masculinity?
your fear of socialism, the big bad monster under the bed?
your belief that poor people just need to
pull harder on their fraying bootstraps?
your greed? oil money? freedom?
the word of fucking god,
who's turned away from us because
you insist that it's only a few bad apples
even though the whole damn orchard is so rotten
that it stinks to high heaven?

this country is built on innumerable corpses,
on oppression wearing freedom's clothes,
and you're the ones keeping the wreck of a thing standing,
the sickly-sweet taste of hypocrisy going rancid in your mouths.
nothing that can be done. can't be helped.
what a shame. thoughts and prayers.

no. fuck that. and fuck you.
you can't build eden without the innocence of childhood:
without having the youngest of our kind be aware enough
to see the world and name its things and wonder,
while still living without the fear of death.
but at the rate we're going, there won't be any such innocents left.

there will only be cain and his blood, marked and killing.
damages sevenfold. exponential grief.
and when the promised paradise eludes us once more,
we with the fingers sullied by divine grief,
whose fault will it be then?

the labyrinth

history a half-man bastard loosed
in daedalus' masterpiece, calling for blood.
ariadne is gone and there is
no way out: penrose steps and
a ceiling open to the stars.
you build wings of wax because you've forgotten
(or you look away from) the past.

history the gorgon with a head of serpents (look away)
and you, clad only in your hubristic, lipophilic death trap,
think you're the one that can conquer her,
even in the face of the innumerable stone men around her cave,
(those who faced goliath before david) names forgotten.

how strange it is that any of us can claim to have
the sole handle on the truth (God is
a pluralism beyond
comprehensibility or nomenclature or selectivity,
so there are no chosen ones, no greater good);
how quickly we forget and let the record of history
skip and repeat skip and repeat and repeat
the same woes over
and over and
over how quickly we forget
and move on and pretend that's forgiveness.

who can but wonder what unsung genius of our time
coming generations will herald;
what those who follow,
godlike, will judge us for?

青春飯

吃青春飯 *means to make the most of one's youthfulness, especially in terms of employment. Literally, "to eat the food of the young."*

over biscuits and slowly cooling pu'er tea,
the adults talking politics national and international,
climate change, religious and racial and cultural clashes.
the kinds of things human beings in the singular
cannot possibly hope to effect change in.

this, they say, sighing into their tea, *is the food of the young*,
resigned as they are to their current stagnancy within
the seemingly still waters of the status quo.
they are floating. that is enough.
pay no attention to the voices below,
slowly losing the fight to gravity, being pulled down
into the depths. pay no attention
to those born out of reach of the waters,
born with a leg up, a silver spoon, a head start.
pay no attention. you are floating.
that is enough.

tomorrow comes to those who wait,
but is sculpted by those who work to shape it in their own image.
you are content because you think you have paid your dues:
put in the work, produced your progeny,
ensured your succession. your future
for whom you sacrificed much. for whom you sacrifice much.

tomorrow is coming, and its seeds
are planted in the fertile grounds of today.
so what are you building? and what will tomorrow bring,
if today's visage is one which
you cannot bear to look at,
let alone take responsibility for?

tomorrow comes to those who wait,
but it is sculpted by those who work to shape it in their own image.
how unfortunate it is that when you cannot see reality
and you fear oblivion,
the image you leave is one which will not reflect
what we need come tomorrow.

did you write all of those dystopias for us
knowing what lay in our future?
to prepare us for the work that had to be done? knowing that this,
this patchwork, threadbare world,
fraying and rotting and barely able to hold its own weight,
which you have left to us as our inheritance,
and the job of picking it apart, burning it to the ground,
and then starting anew, would be left to us, the young?

hymn

in the amber of my memory, my grandmother's house is always hazy with humidity and incense, dimly lit by flickering, bare bulbs. back then, she counted her penance for unknown sins on a clicker, one click for each prayer muttered under her breath: 南無本師釋迦牟尼佛 [click]南無本師釋迦牟尼佛 [click]南無本師釋迦牟尼佛 [click] etcetera. she was training herself, I think; a dog rolling over belly-up, expecting salvation (want a treat?) or perhaps just currying divine favor through sheer numerical power. her attic was a shrine to the gods. the statues in the shadowy alcoves had eyes that followed me around the room and into my nightmares.

she tried early on to save my poor little soul, but I tripped over her prayers and cringed at the smell of incense (see: pavlovian conditioning). for what are gods to a frightened child if not all-powerful, fickle monsters whose whims dictate too much about the world and all its shadows? and besides. what do the divine care for the petty problems of any mere mortal, let alone a mostly-meek-but-occasionally-defiant seven-year-old?

I had a near-crippling need to please back then, but my doubt and desire for tangible results were ultimately victorious in my bitter internal struggle for faith. my godless fear couched itself in terms of impertinence: *what's the point? how can you even be sure that what you're doing works? do the gods even hear you?* the volume of her answering devastation chased me out of the house and into her backyard.

my grandfather found me hiding in the shade of the trees he planted. here was a man who, like me, could no more memorize prayer than he could compose a symphony. I asked him in my fractured Mandarin how his lack of piousness had not gotten in the way of his love for my grandmother, and he laughed. quietly (he was quiet where she was loud), he told me that he had already found the gods. they slept in the earth, he said, but awoke and reached for the heavens in the form of trees and flowers and all things straining against gravity towards the sky.

things feel so final, so permanent as a child. I was seven years old, and God did not walk among the trees for me. nor did they answer my closed-eyed, clasped-handed queries. I was not a good girl for many reasons beyond my borderline-apostasy. but I was still a good enough girl to despair as I declared myself an utter spiritual failure ([dragged between sobs] *i'msorryi'msorry*), doomed to never see the world the way I was raised to.

my grandfather told me that he saw my father in me. he had wandered, said my grandfather, away from the trees and the house that reeked of incense; towards the stained glass and ringing church bells; then towards the temples in the mountains; then away, far away. my father ran an ocean away for breathing space (was it enough?).

my grandmother is forgetting things nowadays. there are days where the incense goes unlit, where she calls my father and asks what time it is and he has to remind her that it is three in the morning here, half a world away (time is only an illusion but distance, distance is what gets you). my grandfather worries, because age is a disease that he cannot prune from this tree.

I don't pray for her. why should I? it's not like my prayers have ever been answered before. but I know my father prays sometimes: head bowed, eyes closed. in his expression I see my grandmother: clicking, counting. I see my grandfather looking at the sky through the treetops. I see a bird with clipped wings, straining to fly. it almost makes me

wish I believed enough in anything to prostrate myself before it with
the hopes I've laid at its feet. to cede control to it.

but god. why should I?

南無本師釋迦牟尼佛 *(námóběnshīshìjiāmóunífó): an invocation of the
name of Buddha Shakyamuni, more commonly known as Siddhārtha Gau-
tama, the founder of Buddhism.*

church

sunshine mischievous peeking through
the fingers of the sequoias
an imperfect silence
settling among the roots of
these trees and their hushed sense
of endless upwardness; the birds
singing hymns in the rafters of this cathedral
built out of photosynthetic defiance against gravity

if you close your eyes and
listen hard enough, you
can hear the heartbeat of the earth
you can hear god speak

revelations

the world is ending and so we dance in the rain
as the seas swallow this sorry excuse for suburbia
we grew up in together; half-submerged now
in the microtonal symphony of waves
crashing over all we've ever known.

smiling so loud my teeth are falling out:
years of stress-related temporomandibular abuse
coming to fruition in this glorious instant
as calcified shards drop from my mouth like sins
or prophecy. the difference being canonization.
but who will remember us now?

right now the world is ending
and we are dancing in the rain,
howling at the moon as it falls from the sky
and laughing at the face of god; what joy there is
in the knowledge that this too shall pass
calamities personal and impersonal alike:
even the fossils you and I become one day will crumble
as the horsemen ride and the sun engulfs
this sorry speck of sentient stardust.

but I am no pillar of salt. I do not look back,
no fondness or sentiment or spite
dragging at my eyes like gravity. no.
I do not look back. you don't either.
there is nothing to be sorry for.
the world is ending. there is nothing left
to be sorry for anymore.

no one is coming to save us. there is no ark
and the prophets are drowning,
cassandra murmuring underwater.
god said *let there be light*
but then cut power to the building
when they didn't want to play anymore.

there is blood on my hands.
yours too, my sister.
whose? doesn't matter.
the rain is washing it away. it doesn't matter.
forget about the aftertaste. it doesn't matter.
the world is ending and we are going to die
dancing hand in hand,
singing over the sound of the wind.

V

"And, while he slaked his thirst, another thirst
Grew; as he drank he saw before his eyes
A form, a face, and loved with leaping heart
A hope unreal and thought the shape was real."

- OVID, METAMORPHOSES (TRANSLATED
BY A.D. MELVILLE)

west of shanghai

you who are carved into
my bones and my heart,
whose name sings through my
veins and swims through
the fog of my mind to
kiss me sweet, you who dreams cannot cage

and neither can my hands, you the most
indelible of berry-juice stains I am
licking off my fingers, whose touch
rolls down my skin
and leaves salt trails in the summer heat.

who knows if I believe in soulmates anymore
but I believe in you,
you who say you think you'll always love me
but I believe you, you who are
improbably impossible,
the luckiest strike of lightning to set me ablaze and who
I pray to everything and anything will strike me again,
you in whose arms I am
the statue of venus, only more or less whole.

you who I tell how I love
so often I have to hold myself back
so the words won't lose their luster,
but no matter how or when I say it
I just lack the eloquence;
neither I nor my words can
hold you for long.

my dearest, my beloved:
there are so many days where I think
it might have been better to have woken up
dead, but then there are the ones where

I wake up in a tangle of limbs
with your breathing twining fingers through my hair
and your heartbeat whispering
the sweetest of nothings in my ear,
you who remind me why I bother.

09.02

imagine this: you're me, and you're in love with this boy, your high
school sweetheart. he is your first love, and at that point, as far as you
are concerned, the love of your life. this boy suddenly suggests that
the two of you go on a walk together. think nothing of it. even though
the two of you rarely venture outdoors without special occasion—your
relationship is based almost entirely around "netflix and chill"-ing in
bed together—jump on the suggestion. take that walk. hell, bring the
dog. dogs are invariably a good idea in any situation. in this particular
situation, the dog can be a focal point with which you can ground
yourself while the love of your life dumps your sorry ass on the sidewalk of his ridiculously white upper-middle class long island neighborhood.

let the absurdity of the situation wash over you. your now-ex is going
on about his rationale behind breaking off your relationship, and it
will undoubtedly be painstakingly thought out. focus on everything
else though, anything but him. the dog is looking for a place to relieve
his bladder. the suburban matriarch of the house you are currently
standing in front of is watering her obscenely color-coordinated
perennials. the hired landscapers meticulously trim the edges of an
already-perfect lawn. the dog has decided the mailbox of this ridiculously picturesque example of a suburban home is not worth his urine.
he is straining at his leash, attempting to continue the walk that has so
suddenly stopped while your now-ex fleshes out his reasoning behind
tearing out your little heart and trampling it underfoot.

there is a poem by william carlos williams about icarus falling into the
sea; how it is springtime so the ploughman goes on ploughing and the
lovely day goes on being lovely, and the drama of icarus drowning is
naught but a splash in the background. perhaps you are drowning, too.

it certainly feels like it. your life as you know it is currently ending, but the jogger up the block keeps jogging and the landscapers keep spreading mulch. the world goes on.

the love of your life, who you suppose is now no longer the love of your life, is still rambling. he is probably saying horribly cliched and melodramatic things; he knows you have always liked that sort of thing. life in general is so much more interesting with a touch of melodrama. right now, though, you just want to leave. you want to go home so you can quickly and violently go through all five stages of grief while eating lactaid ice cream and greasy comfort food. in order to make your getaway, you go through the motions of a breakup conversation, woodenly reciting the same cliches it seems everyone does ("of course we can still be friends"), still feeling all the while that there's no way this is happening to you right now. on today of all days. the second of september: your father's birthday. the universe finds cosmic irony irresistible too, you suppose.

in the messiness surrounding my parents' divorce, my mother lamented often that the twenty years she had spent with my father were for nothing (as a product of those twenty years, I couldn't help occasionally taking that personally). she said that while they were married, she had not seen the kind of person he was. I think it would be more accurate to say that she had blinded herself to the reality of his character, or perhaps that she had denied the truth she saw.

in many ways, we are doomed to follow in the footsteps of our parents. looking retrospectively at the demise of my own relationship, I see cracks where, at the time, I thought we were impenetrable. in truth, I didn't want him as much as I wanted him to change. he didn't have a taste for art or coffee or poetry. he didn't do romance. he didn't know how to deal with my brief but paralyzing periods of depression or my horrible social anxiety. he couldn't take anything seriously. he shamed me for drinking but would himself drink. he was boring in bed. he laughed at my political views. he hated cats.

that being said, I am my mother's daughter, and thus I will happily deny the unpleasant truth until one day, the relationship crumbles in my hands and I am left to wonder what went wrong. as they say, ignorance is bliss. too often we are blind to the failings of the people we love, and too often that blindness is deliberate. hindsight is crystal-clear, but that's only helpful if you can manage to put the relationship behind you.

so imagine this: you're me, and your sorry ass has just been dumped. you and your now-ex take the slightly awkward walk back to his house. the dog (a truly adorable fellow, but not a very smart one) remains entirely oblivious to your emotional devastation. once in the house, you free the excitable pup from his leash and say goodbye, knowing the statistical likelihood of your ever seeing him again is staggeringly low. you head down familiar stairwells and hallways back to your ex's room to grab your keys so you can get the hell out of there. but just before you leave, your ex stops you for one last hug. you've never been good at denying him anything, so you assent. he practically explodes into tears in your arms. you have no fucking idea how to deal with this, so once he kinda sorta gathers himself, you make your escape.

afterwards, you get in your car to drive home. the shock settles in slowly, like a chest cold, building pressure, making you painfully aware of the empty spaces in your body and soul which this relationship had filled for the past two years. when you love someone, they become a part of you—a part that can be beneficial, but it can also be poisonous. how can you possibly live without a part of yourself though? your life is different with them in it and therefore unrecognizable from how it was before, which makes you think that there can be no after. the fact that you survived so long before meeting them makes no difference.

my mother recalled to me once the early days of her relationship with my father. in my view of things, the early days were really the only happy ones. she still thought that man, who couldn't get enough of her, who was quiet and smart and a little shy but sweet as hell, was still in there somewhere, in that shell of a man simmering like a pressure cooker sitting on a roaring fire. or at least she wanted to believe that was the case so badly that it blinded her. so she was of course unhappy. but she never left him.

they say love is blind. but I don't think that's quite right. love is some of the clearest sight there is. insecurities are what blind you. you aren't sure there's anyone else who could ever want you if you left this relationship, so you stay in it and turn a blind eye to the field of red flags. you think you can change this person, but you don't want to admit you have no way of controlling or even fully knowing another person, so you just refuse to add up the signs which signify that the relationship is tanking. you were always mama's special boy, so you can't bear the thought that anything about you is mediocre or flawed, and you blame everything going wrong in your life on the woman who's devoted herself to you for twenty years.

still, love, when done right, makes you better. even if you can never truly plumb all the depths of another person and fully comprehend them. love is still a good thing. maybe you are in love with this person, or maybe you are just in love with your idea of this person or the way they make you feel. does it make a difference? whatever the case, when you are in love, you can do more, be more, be better. the world is a bigger place, but that does not frighten you. the love you feel opens doors and windows.

so it's alright if it ends, as all things do. the relationship has done its job, and you can move on now, with gratitude filling your heart to bursting. the doors are open. the windows are too. the world is a big place. so go on.

be free.

someone new

i: ares

standing in that claustrophobic elevator
with your voice winding fingers
through my hair to whisper in my ear,

the heat of your body palpable
even through the layers of clothing
between us/did you notice
the shiver of desire running down my spine

or how hard it was for me
not to lean into you
or how badly I wanted your hands
to follow your voice
in closing the centimeters between us?

(centimeters between us
and you're still too far away;
I want to map out the topography
of your musculature with my mouth)
there's honey crystallizing in your breath
and citrus rind under your tongue:
is it any wonder I wanted a taste?

ii: apollo

you with your head tilted back in the autumn sun
and something like wonder in your eyes,
telling me that you've never seen
anything like it where you're from: the crisp air,
the smell of sweet decay,
the trees shedding their summer greens in favor of fall colors.

something about the whole thing (you,
the leaves spinning in the wind, the smile
playing shyly around your eyes, your mouth) makes me
want to reach for you, to
anchor you here, to ask you
not to leave me.
useless, futile, I know,
I know, I know, but

I can't help but wonder what could be
if things were different, (if I told you
how often I've been dreaming of you lately,
in colors lovely enough to be rendered by your hands)
if you and I weren't being pulled in opposite directions,
two leaves spinning in the current of the river
and then diverging at the fork.

but of course you can't stay;
life calls and you have to answer
even if that does leave me hanging.
and besides, you don't even have a jacket warm enough
to get you through the winters here.

iii: aphrodite

oh my god, hey! (not to sound cliche
but I want to run every mile of your legs with my tongue,
especially when you're in that dress)
it's so great to see you again, you look amazing!
red really is your color; sets off the undertones of your skin
(god, your skin: I wonder if it tastes like caramel too)
where'd you get it, blah blah blah
(my hands want so badly to run through your hair
that they're trembling) have you done something
different with your hair? you look great (I want
bruises in the shape of my mouth littering the slope of your throat
and the shadows of my fingers imprinted on your hips)

really, you look *so* good (god help me)
that lipstick looks great (I want to *devour* you)
blah blah blah, tell me more (I tell you nothing, but
tell me more)

iv: eros

auguste rodin's hands must have
shaped you, beautiful thing,
creeping ivy twining through my
heart and soul, pulling apart
the bricks of the walls and
letting the light in.

I have been too much in the dark
with you so far and so long away;
I've had no choice but to make you
the stuff of my dreams.

or more accurately, in order to fall asleep,
I need to picture you wrapped around me,
you running fingers over my skin to
feel the bones underneath, me
timing my breathing to yours,
listening to your heartbeat.

maybe it's too soon to say
but I've been thinking about
things that last lifetimes and wondering if
you would be so kind as to
stay awhile?

v: poseidon

under the amber lights of the bar,
your eyes deep sea just out of reach of the sun
when you were in a suit and I was
drunk and trying to keep from
running my fingers along the inner seam of
your trousers and licking the taste of whiskey
out of your mouth, and the only thing that stopped me
was that I hate the taste of whiskey.

but god, those eyes: I think a lot about
drowning myself, and the seas of your eyes
seem as good a place as any to die.
better, even (come now, darling; die a little with me).
you brooding tempest, you maelstrom, you
dark chocolate temptation, sweet as wine
melting under the movement of my tongue,
your eyes squeezing shut and seas rushing down my throat.

sapphic

Sappho: Archaic Greek lyric poet. widely regarded in ancient times as one of the greatest lyric poets. She was given epithets such as "the Tenth Muse" and "the Poetess." Most of Sappho's poetry has been lost; her extant works are largely fragmentary. She is known for writing about, among other things, the trials and tribulations of love, particularly with women. Hence, the common usage of the word "sapphic" to describe a woman who loves women.

i: aphrodite

under the bench swing
tangled in each other and tasting
dying a little death
the taste
the dampness
of breath and eyes squeezed shut,

your brother walked in
slipping my hand up your shirt
tied in too many knots to jump apart

ii: hera

on the leather couch
your childhood home
you taste like pineapple.
I lick it from both ends of your lips
you beg me
stop before you scream your siblings awake.

enveloped in your warmth
want to sleep with my head on
your tender breast
at least til morning comes

iii: helen

excuse my staring:
you're wearing too much eyeliner
I've been drinking too much,

by the time the sun rises
your name escapes me
the taste of you won't
(jack and coke and lipstick)

iv: muses

in loving you,
either I give
or you take or both and then I'm
empty and by morning

you're gone

divine

i

you're not really my type or anything, but
when you dance I always picture
me rolling you around on my tongue,
you writhing above me,
and the taste of your wanting seeping down my throat.

your hair is its own continent unconquered
and I want to plunge my exploratory fingers
into its depths like the promise of more.
something about the stretch and pull of your muscles
feels worth prayer, as in:
o morning star, shining bright on the brow of the old titan,
I run to you, heedless of my waxen cartilage melting.
for you I fall apart gladly. for you I fall apart.
take this blood for it is of my body,
an offering before your glory.
take me, burn me, let me
rise to you as smoke and let you breathe me in.

ii

the ancients thought the sun was a god
(or goddess, we aren't picky here) and as such
did not dare look it in the eye. you've seen dogs, wolves, yes?
when you submit to someone (laying on your back
with everything vital about you exposed) you are no longer
on their level and thus unworthy of such contact.

and yet sometimes we peek anyway,
give in to that addict itch
to visually caress the curves of their faces.
perhaps for a ménage à quarte
(eye fucking, I think the kids call it these days)
if the mood is right; it doesn't matter if it's
the road out of hades, I want need have to see you,
even if it's only once and you're gone and it's my fault you're gone

and then nature itself will weep as I sing
and I'll welcome with open arms the maenads that tear me apart.
but search my entrails all they like,
they won't find my heart, because that belongs to you.
and finally, in death, I'll come home to you.

I just had to see you
forgive me, love.
I couldn't help myself.

iii

a fuckboy? who, me?
no, I'm not like that.
I mean, yeah, I'll want you until you want me
and then play with you until I get tired and want to discard you
but I can't find a bin anywhere, and I'm not gonna litter;
I'm not a complete fucking asshole.
I'll carry you until I can dispose of you properly
but I'll be real annoyed about it the whole time.

definitely still an asshole though,
let me make that abundantly clear.
the thrill is in the chase, you know?
the journey, not the destination.
no, scratch that. I enjoy coming
to my destination as much as anyone else.

so a better metaphor: the battle, and the victory.
the conquest.
and this is guerilla warfare, of course.
it's madness to run headlong into enemy territory
with your heart on your sleeve, cards out for all to see.

no, I lay linguistic snares and wait for you to come by,
unsuspecting of my less-than holy intentions.
I tell you I'll write you immortal and glorious,
sing your praises, tell your lies.
my words wrapping around you, wrapped
around my little finger.

come on, babe,

it'll be fun.

shall I compare thee to a summer's day?

devotion

i

in asian mythology they say those who
take their own lives will be condemned
to a purgatorial eternity replaying their ill-gotten deaths
over and over and over again. you kill yourself to end
the pain but it only makes the pain eternal.

everything changes but death. sisyphus hauling the boulder
up the cliff and throwing himself off the edge
only to wake up at the bottom
with the taste of blood in his mouth
and god laughing
and a new boulder to carry.

every day the same. wake
eat sleep fuck you play work
fuck me despair work eat sleep
wake fuck work ugh fuck work
sleep wake eat. to advance,
to move on, to end the monotony,
you kill yourself kill yourself kill yourself
kill yourself kill yourself over and over and over and over and

ii

there's an apartment in nanjing.
gulou district. shiziqiao. sixth floor.
the third floor of the building is a hotpot restaurant,
the smells stewing in the elevator,
which trembles in anticipation.
or maybe that's me. are the lights flickering?

there's a keypad on the door of the apartment.
what's the code? can't remember.
I step inside somehow anyway.
I climb up the ladder-like stairs

to the loft. most of the space is eaten up
by a memory foam mattress on the floor. so big a third of it
folds against the wall, making the thing L-shaped.
one power strip crammed into the tiny sliver of floor beside it.
if you're sleeping, your glasses might be there too.
a discarded shirt. the contents of your pockets.
if not, you might be sitting up against the abused third of your mattress,
waiting. your eyes your mouth your body would smile on seeing me.

there are days where I live for that smile.
I don't tell you that. I never would.
(even though my despondent mental mantra of
killyourselfkillyourselfkillyourselfkillyourself
marches onward ever onward)
instead I smile back. ask you about your day.
slide into the warmth of your bed and you and your love.

or. not love. we don't call it love.

I didn't know until later that you felt anything at all.

this was just about the sex for me.

and about breaking the monotony.

wake eat school work eat ((despair)) sleep

wake eat school work eat ((despair)) sleep

turns to wake eat school fuck work ((despair)) sleep

wake eat school fuck work ((despair)) sleep

because it's just sex. it helps. a little. it's just sex.

at first. then it wasn't. and I, in this moment,

am worried that it is for you. just about the sex, I mean.

regardless of how you feel, we're in your apartment

and I'm burning with this thing,

so close to love it might be love but might not

but may as well be, welling up under my tongue,

words grasping the gates of my teeth with desperate hands

to keep from being forced out, dropped into your lap

like an outdoor cat bringing you half-dead things.

iii

gulou district. it is late. or early.

a matter of perspective.

I am going home. not my home, but home.

my apartment is also on the sixth floor.

but unlike yours, mine is a walk-up in a residential area

with no streetlights. no night guards.

no restaurants or street vendors.

no witnesses. every time I walk home,

I wonder about your reaction to my death.

you would be sad, of course.

perhaps you would blame yourself.

my sister too, poor thing. but with 7,340 miles

and ten months of distance on top of a 13-hour time difference,

she barely feels like anything more than a fictional character to me now.

still.

the thought of hurting someone else

keeps me from making the walk to the yangtze

and submitting to the ancient depths.

or from stepping in front of one of the few cars passing at the hour.

or consolidating my remaining six months of antidepressants into one dose.

or putting my sturdiest belt to a weight test. the endless possibilities,

halted.

later, when you live in shanghai
(a bigger apartment on the third floor.
I stay with you on the weekends.
when you first moved in we played house
and fucked in every room of it.)
I will think the same morbid thoughts
(*killyourselfkillyourselfkillyourselfkillyourself*)
on the platform of the bullet train
and while waiting for the subway
and on the ever-darkening roads home from the station.

but I don't know that yet.
I just know that you are asleep in your shiziqiao apartment
and you want me to text you when I get home.
how easily I could lie to you.

but as I leave your apartment, I always say
I will. and the unspoken promise includes
not just *getting home*, but also *safe*.

iv

there's an apartment in nanjing.
gulou district. shiziqiao. sixth floor.
there's a half-dead thing that's been left on the doormat.
you open your door and let it in.

the wounded thing sits on your bed.
you have your hand clamped over its knee.
it is somehow perched on the edge of a seat,
though the loft is too small to house a chair.
it seems to be considering bolting.
assessing exit routes. furtively looking you over.
calculating outcomes. who would win.
it trembles. in fear? pain?

you're in your apartment
and there's an elephant in the room.
you and the wounded thing meticulously
avoid making eye contact with the giant
living secret. your conversation
steps carefully around it.
you studiously ignore the way
the apartment has shifted to accommodate it.

you look back at what you found on your doorstep,
what you brought into your home.
is it half-dead or half-alive?
the room is filling with the smell of blood
and secrets so loud they threaten to crack your floors.

you want to ask what brings it here.
the wounded thing. and the elephant it brings.
you know that you should not.
that the answer will cleave apart
the sturdy house of your heart.
but something (the voice of reason?
or a poacher in reason's clothes?)
makes you open your mouth.
those scars, you say.

did you do that to yourself?

V

there's an apartment in nanjing.
gulou district. shiziqiao. sixth floor.
the neighbors have transitioned over the weeks
from knocking on the walls when we fuck
to fucking loudly as well.
we joke about congratulating them
with a gift basket of condoms.

meanwhile I am the demon and the possessed and
expected to be the exorcist as well
but I am so tired. the ((despair)) is
a boulderweight on my strained bones

and you can make me forget for a while.
it's a lot harder to come by drugs in china
so. this.

sometimes if I orgasm hard enough
I can pretend I really am finally dying.
that I don't have to live anymore with the ((despair))
fighting to consume me from the inside out.
la petite mort, indeed. a lovely substitute.
or at least enough to get me by for now.
for the most part.

vi

there's an apartment in nanjing.
you have slit the throat of
the elephant in the room.
or maybe I have. I'm the one with
the razors, after all.

thinking back, I must have known it would happen.
even cooking knives require a license here.
I had packed some in my checked luggage to bring.
small, single-edged razors. I must have known it would happen.
that I would need to cut open my skin like a pressure release valve
to keep me from being the death of myself.

but we are here, in your apartment.
one of your hands on my knee.
the other desperately struggling to get a grip.
failing. you practically explode into tears.

you told me once you have cried
only three times since childhood.
the last being after a phone call a few weeks ago.
the cancer metastasizing in your friend's brain.
when he could still talk,
he'd begged you to come home and see him.
but you stayed. and so.
listening to his last rites over the phone.

I can't get another phone call, you gasp,
breaths dragged in between sobs.
I can't. I can't. please don't do this please
I CAN'T and I just don't know what to do.

what to say.
I was just trying not to hurt anybody else.
I didn't realize. I'm sorry.
cliché after cliché bubbles up under my tongue
and withers before it passes through my teeth.
I just can't believe your tears are being shed over me.

and maybe I've just gotten too used to this over the years
and I've forgotten that most people don't do this.
see poison in their very souls
and cut themselves open to let it out.
like medieval doctors bleeding their patients.
attempt to exorcise demons with a blood sacrifice.

vii

in an apartment in nanjing
(or was it the one in shanghai?)
you told me you didn't love me.
that you were just a step away from it.
that in every way other than the label,
this was a relationship. you and me.
meandyou.

at the time, my thoughts and words were all
blurring together, the sleep medication I'd taken
stuffing my skull with cotton. so forgive me
if I misremember the wording.
I'm not even sure if I responded beyond
a loopy semblance of a smile. incoherently, undoubtedly.
but even then, my weaving winding circling swaying thoughts
could piece together enough to know you were bluffing.

it makes me smile even now
thinking of how hard you tried not to love me.
you knew from the start that
death was always standing in my peripheral vision
and you were too smart to make such a poor investment.
and yet.

in an apartment we've made your home away from home,
you said you didn't love me.
but what is the power that compels you to weep
for the pain of someone else
if not love?

a pyromaniac's last love letter

my dearest, my love:

I've always loved fire,
have always been tempted
to run my fingers over its soft curves
like a lover. to let it hurt me
like a lover. to let the pain
leave mementos on my skin.

some days I crave this destruction. other times I crave another.
either way, don't talk to me before I've had my morning violence.
this violence of undoing. I crave. like air. like water. like love.
the line between love and hate
infinitesimally thin; the line between love and violence
even thinner.

those times, I want my bruised knuckles rusting,
my wounds weeping life. here with you,
I want the taste of blood (mine or yours?) flooding
my mouth as I kiss you, more teeth than love.
because the anger is a familiar face,
one of the few which can materialize
from the haze of my sadness. my numbness.
a match striking in the darkness for a moment
before burning itself out.
and I want it. because it feels like
something.
so yes. I'm angry. I love you.
I'm angry. are you angry
at me? with me? for me?

I don't think we're meant to be
like this, animals stripped of their former wild glory
and tameness forced upon them.
growling and straining at our leashes. eyes hungry.
but that's what happens when you want me
to cut myself down to size, and I want you
to be more. I want my idea of you/not you,
and you vice versa.

and we both know it isn't fair.
aren't you bored? aren't you in pain?
isn't there that part of you screaming to be free?
come, darling, I'd love to say.
let's go a few rounds.

what stops me is knowing that
the cycle of violence, once started, does not stop
until someone decides
to stop it.

so, my love,
I'm leaving. here is the bridge soaked in fuel,
and here is the match, leaving my hand.
you on one end,

me on the other. each with matching
black eyes and split lips. each with our own
contusive brass knuckles. I'm leaving,
and I think you'll agree it's for the best.
the bridge between us going up in flames.
and us grinning through the pain of it,
blood painting a glaze over our teeth.

besides, the destruction I actually crave most
is that of self. that of wildfire
burning away dead brush to make way for new life,
the ashes of the old feeding the new.
the scar tissue of the land able to breathe again.

so I'm angry. I'm leaving. I'm angry.
I'm angry because it's better than being sad,
and because I love fire so much that perhaps,
if I self immolate, I will finally learn to love myself.

goodbye, ~~my~~ dearest. perhaps we'll see each other again someday
after we've been molded and fired into something new.
or perhaps not. whatever the case,
keep an eye out for smoke in the distance.

~~yours~~
~~truly~~
~~best wishes~~
love,
[an illegible signature, smudged with ash.]

VI

*"Oh, now I know for sure
The image is my own; it's for myself
I burn with love; I fan the flames I feel."*

- OVID, METAMORPHOSES (TRANSLATED
BY A.D. MELVILLE)

nomenclature

i

there is an arboretum twenty minutes from my childhood home
where the trees are sorted by type and labeled
with little metal placards. here is
the pinetum, the juniper, the oak.
here are their latin names, in case you care.
here is a third name in quotation marks,
the significance of which I've never discerned
(nicknames? pet names? calling names?).
here are the little fences we put around the trees (for their safety
or for ours?) and here is the neatly manicured lawn
that surrounds them, with gravel paths that cut through it. this is nature
compiled. curated. sanitized. safe.

I'm not sure why there are three or more names
on each placard. it's one tree, one thing;
but we are struggling with clarity, for we must
be clear here what we mean what we know
what we intend. or perhaps what they the tree intend.
we want to know. we want things to be
fixed, sewn into the firmament
with boundaries defined, because then
we need not search,

because the idea of chaos reigning is just too much.
the forest unknown, rooted and teeming with
life and intelligence and meaning
which we cannot fully discern in the deep shadows.
the barely-there paths fading out of sight.
we, the ones who are not rooted, are afraid.
we wanderers fear the chaos. so. the labels.

but the tree knows itself without us. the tree needs not
a label in human tongues dead and alive transcribed.
it knows itself without us. it *is* without us.
the placard is for our viewing convenience only,
as is the fence and the path and the lawn
picked clean of weeds.

ii

how many times have I been asked
where are you ~~really~~ from? and not known how to answer?

they don't want to hear that I was born and raised here,
that english may not be my mother tongue
but my mother tongue withered in my childhood mouth
because my parents moved us to a white suburban neighborhood
and wanted us to practice speaking a language
our neighbors would understand.

when they ask that question, they want to hear the *erhu* in my throat singing
the songs of my people from three thousand years ago
or a peking opera about us running from the communists
so that we wouldn't be left bleeding out in tiananmen
or fighting the persistent trash in the street
for a *hukou* in shanghai (never mind that
my parents have never set foot in mainland china,
that their childhood was spent under the martial law
of a government that saw communists and traitors in every shadow,
terror so stark it was white).
these people don't look at me and think *american*,

because my face is my placard is my label is me,
and if they think american and don't think of me,
then there's no way I could be american.
it doesn't matter if *I* think of myself as american
or if I cut open my veins to show them how similar our blood is.

all they see is the difference. and they are frightened
by the difference, by the unknowns it suggests.
the world is bigger than they thought and it frightens them.
people are more complicated than they thought
and it frightens them.

iii

what does it matter to you, who I love or lust for,
the sex I am or the sex I'm having?
haven't you ever considered that it's just
none of your goddamn business?
have you ever even once entertained the thought
of minding your own goddamn business,
instead of trying to draw all these boxes and labels and lines
and writing those arbitrary scribbles into language and law

and calling it the word of god? haven't you considered
that god made me the way I am and that
you are not god cannot judge cannot hold me,
and that your word your law might be a misinterpreted mistranslation
of ineffable divine murmurings, a bad game of telephone
stretching across millennia devolving;
that to think you are not just another blind man
groping for the shadow of the elephant on the wall of the cave
is hubris?

iv

don't ask me how I identify. I don't know.
I know that I love easily and fast,
briefly and violent. I know that my love
always expects more out of people than they can give;
that my love is never fair, is always war.
I know that words are slippery things, bloated with
not just their dictionary definitions but also
their sociopoliticocultural implications.

so I don't know. gay? bi? pan? queer?
and hell. pronouns? she? they? I don't fucking know.
I love without regard to gender or sex, sure,
and I guess I'm comfortable enough in my given body most of the time,
but nothing ever fits quite right, the walls of the boxes
closing in, the claustrophobia limiting constricting
flattening simplifying suffocating

comforting. for some anyway.
complexity and unknowns are too much for most.
but I? (*I'm not like other girls*) I wallow in
negative capability, the gray areas among gray areas.
I hate poetry with a palpable design upon me, mr. keats,
and just want it to be a thing which enters into one's soul
and does not startle it or amaze it with itself.

ambiguity is a comfort to I who feel labels as chains.
who resents the metal placard for allowing mere passerby
to think they can know me.
who is a tree which, given time, will grow
even after a fence has been wired around its trunk.
will grow beyond the fence. will consume the fence
within the unbelievable expansionary force of its being.

medusa with the head of perseus

Sculptor Luciano Garbati created Medusa with the Head of Perseus *in 2008, depicting a reversal of the Greek legend wherein Medusa is slain by Perseus. Garbati's sculpture has been linked to the Me Too movement.*

the fantasies of daphne crowning the brow of the sun,
of leda and the swan, of all the women fucked by gods and
men who could not keep their hands to
themselves: revenge the lesser, the greater being
not to be weaponized, known only in your name.
known only by my body.

me too means yes let there be light
shed on the crimes of those who would silence us
but also see me, too. I am a survivor of cataclysm and more
I am a survivor I am a cataclysm I am more.

medusa had a mortal champion come to meet her
and so she took the chance which the others could not:
to prove to her tormentors that she too
is a hunter. that death is not just for prey.
that it will come for you too. that fear
is not just for me but also you too.
she brandishes her trophy
and looks the gods in the eyes and says

look here/hear me: here
is your champion and here I am too.
you raped me in the temple of a virgin goddess
and she made it such that you nor anybody else
could ever again look me in the eye
but I was still a prize to be won over
by shows of violence nonetheless.
yet here is your champion. and here I am.

so where has that left us?
he will be another notch on my bedpost,
another stone where there was once a man. and you
will be left with the taste of a warning in your mouth:
death comes for us all. judgement comes for us all.
even gods. even you.

chinadoll

I am five years old and shy to the point of pain, but
still know to dig in my heels when I am right.
the stereotype of my people (*yellow*, as if
dandelion sunshine canary is closer to my truth) is head bowed
over schoolwork, tongue bitten into silence,
eyes near closed in concentration.
I am the model minority (and if that is untrue
my eyes are squinted too hard to see) I am I am.

but my parents did not leave their roots behind
and start anew in a new place with new tongues and new faces
just so they could raise model children. no.
I am shy to the point of pain. but I still have a spine.

there is a boy in school that calls me a chinadoll while
belittling my slanted eyes with nursery rhyme fluency:
ching chong chinadoll, can you even see?
and even though I learned to read at two I do not have the vocabulary
as a kindergartener to tell him in so many words
to *fuck the fuck off*, but I find that
I cannot be quiet head down eyes nearly closed
with the effort of unseeing, which is what
leads to me dragging him behind a row of shelves and trying

to beat the shape of my unsayable words into his skin.
he hits me back and I answer louder and his bruises echo
and we trade blows until the teacher drags me off of him.

I tongue my split lip, the cracked edges of Qing porcelain,
and taste my iron sweet blood.

overripe

a vignette: my mother in a Chinese supermarket
fruit or vegetable cupped
in the curvature of her palm or
wrapped in her lightly callused fingers

the click-tap metronome of
fingernails on fruit or vegetable skin
slightly irregular as she listens
to what it tells her: whether or not
it is ready to martyr itself (take this bread
for it is my body) to nurture herself and her children.

but towards the end, my father would not stand
to be touched by her. maybe that was
why his leaving came as such
a surprise to her; she could not
lean in close and cup him
in her hands and listen
to the hollowness within.

even as a child, though
I could see the bruises on their marriage:
the rot, the souring; and I wonder
how my mother did not see

(or if she simply refused to see)
that this fruit was slowly
turning to poison, sickening her
and her children.

and her husband, too
I suppose; her lover of twenty years who
did not love her (didn't she know
that just because this man planted
his seed in her gardens to grow
it did not mean he was good for her
or deserved her?).

mother of my blood, please:
the fruit on the table is attracting flies.
throw it out. take out the trash.
open the windows.

breathe in the spring-sweet air,
no longer laden with decay.
listen to the sounds of birds,
the rejoicing of new beginnings.
go on now. you're finally free.

nanking

she is golden, gleaming, garbage.
sodden with humidity and trampled by the masses,
mildew creeping up the eaves, and yet
beautiful, of course.
a city as beautiful as a painted harlot.

when you see the golden city caught in the throes of dusk,
her face lit up in ecstasy, know that
only she knows if it's real (why do men
even ask if you've come when the real question
is whether or not you'll swallow
your disappointment) and if you've fallen in love with her,
then you're a fool, you poor thing.

and if for some reason you think she loves you, then
you're irredeemably lost: her body is her weapon
(here is the flytrap; here is the spider) and
you can pretend all you like that you can conquer her,
but in the end you are nothing special:
she remains and you are subsumed within her,
another face among millions, doomed
to one day feed the grass and the slow-moving rivers,
your bones set into the foundations
of the next generation as they build to the skies;
as she moves on and forgets you.

I thought once that loving you was woven into my muscle fibers,

an expression of divine grace laced through

my ribcage, holding me together, but it turns out

my associations between places and faces

are too strong to disentangle as I leave her/you/now,

(we two bewildered travelers in a foreign land:

I'm sorry for expecting more from you

when I can barely manage enough object permanence

to remember that even now, you are real)

and I'm only ever in love conceptually,

since nobody is enough of an abstraction for me.

yes, my dear, I'm leaving.

no, dear, it's not you; it's me

I'm looking for

love language

traditional japanese breakfasts are hearty affairs:
soup and rice and vegetables and fish
for which someone must rise very, very early,
put on an apron, wash their hands, and begin.

sometimes you prepare parts of it the night before,
but freshness is a virtue. and who wouldn't love waking
to the smell of fresh rice, the sizzle of salmon,
the feel of natto sticking as your chopsticks swirl,
the richness of miso soup wrapping you in its fragrant arms?

alongside breakfast, they make お弁当,
meticulous and stuffed to the brim
(with love) for their spouses and children and selves.
made with an eye for portion control, but also color coordination.
balancing aesthetic and taste. tempura alongside heart-shaped carrots.
tamagoyaki cut into flower shapes and animal faces made of sesame seeds.
fried fish luscious with tartar sauce. boxed up,
wrapped in cloth, now run along. 行ってらっしゃい!
spelling without words *see how I love you? heart and soul.*

if the eyes are the windows to the soul,
then the mouth is the way to the heart.
but the japanese know that you eat with both.
you say your thanks before the meal, knowing
you are loved. heart and soul.

I wish I was my subject of my love poems. the real ones,
~~where it's not about me but you~~ where it's the love talking
and not the lust or the loneliness trying to get a word in edgewise.

I wish I felt I deserved the best of myself,

that the best of myself belonged to me first.

that I would stop giving so much of myself

to people I've convinced myself I love so much.

so much that there is little to nothing left for me.

really, I just want to love someone enough

(heart and soul) to happily wake up early every morning

so I can make them お弁当.

even though I'm not a morning person.

even if it's just myself.

お弁当 *(obento): bento box/a Japanese box lunch.*

行ってらっしゃい *(itterasshai): Have a good day/Take care! Usually said*
to someone leaving the house. Literally, "go, and come back".

april

while on a walk the other day
I saw tulips blooming in a planter box and I almost cried
right then and there, on the crowded sidewalk.

I never used to be this emotional,
but nowadays anything gets me going:
shattered glass on the pavement, catching the light
as it drains out of the sky at sunset;
videos of dogs waiting for someone to come home;
numbers on a scale, measuring
how much space I take up;
dollars in my wallet, phasing
in and out of existence;
the sight of new green buds
sprouting from the dead-looking trees.

you see, every winter my love for this city
withers and dies along with the broadleaf trees.
I forget why I love it here
or why I bother staying.
when it rains when they said it would snow
and the sleet mixes with the salt on the pavement,
the slush that forms on the sidewalk
seeps into my shoes and
under my skin.

I forget
because it's easier than
torturing myself with the memory
of the new york sun that
comes and goes (all summer in a day),
easier than going mad with grief
at the sight of that cold, dying star
trapped behind the gridlocked clouds,
struggling to light up this freezing concrete wasteland.

in the winter,
I lie dormant under the frozen earth,
curled in fetal position among
the tangled roots of bare trees.
forgetting the sun
and the warmth
and how to be alive.

but april comes like a long lost lover
and exhumes me;
she sweeps me up in her tumultuous moods
and holds me close.

and the gardeners in this gentrified neighborhood:
they wake the waiting dormant bulbs
thawing in the softening earth,
and me along with them.
and I remember.

I remember the smell of spring rain.
I remember greens and pinks and yellows that
the winter gray had bleached from my memory.
I remember that no matter
how long and bitter the winter is,
the flowers and trees all still know
how to bloom again when spring comes.

maybe I have forgotten how to do the same.
or maybe not.

maybe the seed and the root
are still there.
somewhere.

waiting for the sun.

quota

forget talking about sex: I wish
someone had sat me down when I was younger to tell
my unformed self you do not have to be anything. love
is not transactional conditional contractual.
your voice is worth hearing and you do not have to be anything.
you do not have to be good. your voice is worth hearing.
you do not have to be good. you are worth loving.

instead I had to learn things the hard way,
knees scraped to scar tissue from all the times I've fallen down

down

down

into the arms of someone who loved me
to bruises to pieces to death (if someone wants you
but only if you change, then they don't want you. they want
their idea of you which is smaller than you.
do not cut yourself down to size. do not
contort yourself to fit within the boundaries
of their expectations, lest ye one day
open your eyes to find you are
unable to stand up straight again.)

and it's hard.
so hard. to put yourself back together again
after you built up your walls and then had a great fall
(or was it the other way around?) but it's okay.
it's hard. but it's okay.
you live and you learn and you fall
and you bleed and cry and scream and pray for something to change
and it will.

it will. change is the way of things,
just as sakura bloom and wilt and death and birth.
even if things don't go your way. they will change.
you will change. you do not have to be anything.

they will change. maybe you can find it in yourself to love them still,
or maybe you can't and it's okay. it's all okay.
you do not have to be anything and neither do they.
look after yourself. you do not have to be good,

but you should still look after yourself,
because someone should. you are worth loving,
even if you are not loved. you are still worth it.
you do not have to be good. you are still worth it.

listen, darling:
if you only have so much love to give,
make sure that at the end of the day,
some of you still belongs to yourself.

living

the love I feel for this city extends to you,
random passerby or bus driver or stranger whose apartment curtains are open,
as you float by me with a snippet of incomprehensible conversation
or live your life at home as if unobserved and unobserving. I love you
just a little and I don't know you and I love you. I love you anyway,
just a little, for living in this moment
and crossing my path. it is always in these moments that I think

that my relationship with life, tiresome as it may be at times,
is worth trudging on through, no matter how uncertain
the footing: seeing a phonebound pedestrian's eyes
crinkle with private foreign laughter;
watching someone patiently watch the traffic signals change;
wincing as a would-be passenger fumbles with their metro card.

life turns to me with laughter in her tired eyes,
a hand held out to me like promised salvation.
it's the little things about her: her smell,
her touch, her sound. the very experience
of being with her. in her.

a dogwalker, preoccupied as god,
struggling to keep their seven charges from greeting me;
a bewildered tourist asking for help
deciphering the hieroglyphics of a subway map;
a couple walking as one entity through the park,
their eye contact an entire language I cannot speak.

after the honeymoon phase of our relationship,
wherein I was swept up in the anxieties of new love
and fragile childhood, I got tired of her.
and she of me? I know not. I know only that
I spent too much time looking into the dark eyes of death,
wondering if perhaps I could drown there.
flirting, perhaps. life and I fought a lot then.
but I still loved her, somewhere. somehow.
and I still do.

when the man in the deli wraps up a bagel
(eggeverythingbaconegg&cheese) with practice-swift certainty;
when the occupants of a child-laden stroller
cover their ears, faces scrunched, as an ambulance wails by;
when the memories of movement and life and the heartbeat of the city
emanate up through the subway grates in the sidewalk.

it is in these moments when I am in love
that I turn to life and apologize
for taking her for granted. for trying
to drive her away. we both know death
wouldn't let me fall in a moment's love
with strangers just for living this life alongside me
for only the briefest glancing blow of an intersection.
it's too jealous for even that.

the poet

i

li bai, the greatest of chinese poets,
died like this: the emperor tang daizong
named the poet the registrar of the left commandant's office
but when the imperial edict found him in anhui,
he was already dead and had been for some time.
the 詩仙, the poet immortal, mortal no longer;
returned from whence he came, perhaps.

despite the fame of this poet-more-than-man,
there was and is and will be always
disagreement on how he met his end.
some say the poet immortal, the wine immortal,
drank himself to death.
others say the rot in his lungs took him,
the vise of disease dragging him into its suffocating embrace.

but still others say he, drunk as was his wont one night,
took his boat out to the yangtze river
and tried to embrace the white jade plate of the moon
reflected in the deep-moving waters.

how many versions of your death would you like there to be?
or perhaps a better question is:
how shrouded in myth would you like to become?
how ambiguous would you like to be?
or maybe: how easily do you want people
to be able to grasp you?

ii

manic depression and an impressionist painting style
ahead of its time walk into a bar.
or perhaps an artist. or perhaps a man.

the madness lowers its lashes and voice in tandem,
flirting with the art. the art is unable to remain unaffected.
and the bar/artist/man is swept over with emotion

which can only be released in streaks of oil on canvas,
piecing together a whole made more than itself,
infinitely greater than the sum of its parts.

vincent van gogh is perhaps the platonic ideal
of a tortured artist. think yellow paint,
self-mutilation. social ostracism and

mental institutions with a view.
captured on canvas. for all to see.
struggling clawing fighting

for success for sanity for love.
for a semblance of stability.
for the art which so inspires joy even now

to bring him peace.
there's an episode of doctor who
where the time travelers bring van gogh

to a museum dedicated to him.
showing his success, the praise of his genius.
the awe of the crowds. the masses. the world.

and then after he goes back to his time,
they go back to the museum to see if things have changed
for the better. but they find out

he still shot himself.
he set his heart ablaze and
poured his molten soul out onto canvas

and then died by his own hand.
a thousand cliches come to mind:
those who burn brightest burn out first;

he was commissioned by god to paint
the bright vaults of heaven;
etcetera. when I was younger,

I thought this a good life lived.
god gives you the talent to channel your curse
and you burn the wick of yourself straight to the end.

you die alone, unknown, unsuccessful.
but then you are worshiped in the annals of history.
your suffering given purpose. your death for our sins.

you have fulfilled your purpose.
your happiness does not matter.
                    or does it?

iii

as a preteen preoccupied with perceiving
and being perceived, I was too mired in myself
to write for anyone but myself.
an audience unwelcome. of one. for one.
my room full of composition notebooks
comprised of unseen thoughts made visible
and then folded back in on themselves
like self-satisfied birds.

the life of an artist is a fickle one,
subject to the fluctuational whimsy of
the public eye, ever-roving. do you know me
or know me not. do you love me
or love me not. will I die alone and known
or unknown and unloved. terribly exhausting,
the consciousness of one being watched.

being overly preoccupied with death
and with myself and how I was perceived
distracted me from the work, though.
I wanted to be a poet, not write poetry.
not make art. not do the work.
I wanted to die, and I wanted it to be
grimy and lovely and romantic.

now, however, it does not matter.
none of it does: not me. not my death.
since it is with the gradual degradation
of a bouquet of flowers (mortifying, wilting, gone)
that I write myself out of existence

and into eternity. ambiguous and immortal.
dead and lovely and undying. as art is to be.

that is the hope. perhaps.
that you, the beholder,
gaze upon what I lay before you
and feel. some art is the storm,
tearing its way rampant through your cluttered soul
and leaving you afterwards
battered and bereft. but clean.

other art hits like the gasp of air
which the nearly-drowned
scrabble at with desperate fingernails
and waterlogged panic. you flailing,
dragging at the artist with a bruising grip
which begs them to save you please just
save me help me oh god please no I'm—

but some art is just this:
a quiet room.
you are curled up, perhaps,
on a cozy sofa by the window. reading.
a soft secret of a smile
steals its silent way across your face
and you glance up, looking out the window.

you marvel in the gentle sun,
the sounds of life. warmth curls in your chest,
slow and content as a sleepy cat.
you are alive. you are alive,
and it is lovely. you are lovely.
the art lives in you, alive and beholding,

in you and in the space between you and the artist
whether they are here or there or anywhere
or feeding the fish at the bottom of the yangtze;
whether they speak in rhyme or on canvas
from across millennia or centuries
or a couple of minutes while you're brewing a cup of tea.
it doesn't matter. it is lovely. and you are lovely,
alive and here and now.

Acknowledgments

―――――

If you've gotten this far in my book, I'd like to thank you. It's been hard, I imagine. This was hard to write, hard to share, and hard to be brave about. But I did it with the hopes that I've cleared the air, so to speak. Or perhaps I've cleared a path for you to have your own hard conversations and searches and creative endeavors. And, of course, to hopefully do it while being as supported as I am fortunate to have been.

There have been many points in my life where I've felt alone, but the process of making this book into a reality has thankfully and mercilessly reminded me again and again that I am not only not alone, but also surrounded by many, many wonderful people, for whom my written gratitude will forever seem to me inadequate. But no matter; the people who have walked this path with me did not do so for the sake of thanks. I'll still take a moment to name a few, however.

To Regina Stribling, Ashley Lanuza, Natalie Botero, and the rest of the editorial team: The real work of writing isn't mere creation. In truth, the bulk of it is editing. This book would have remained a mess of notes and sketches squirreled away in my various notebooks and on my phone if not for your tireless work, thoughtful feedback, and occasional battles with my insecurities. Thank you for putting up with my nitpicking and for helping me shape this book into something I'm truly proud of.

To Anthony Edwards, Janette Wu, Alice Tsai, and Yvonne Ma: I say I wrote this book for myself, but that isn't strictly true, and we all know it. Thank you for making sure that my rambling, semi-coherent thoughts are comprehensible to someone who isn't trapped in my mind at all times, for giving me your valuable input and kind words, and for being friends I trust enough to show an unfinished, unpolished version of my heart.

To the team at NDP and the Creator Institute and especially to Professor Eric Koester: I've said it before, and I'll say it once more. I'll forever be grateful that you gave me the opportunity and resources to make one of my life's biggest dreams since childhood come true. Thank you, thank you, again and again.

To my family: This book is, at its core, a documentation of my journey towards understanding and loving myself. You've been a big part of that process, and thus part of who I am today. Thank you for being my biggest supporters through the best and worst of times. I never would have been able to take a risk like this without being secure in the knowledge that no matter what, I have you all. I hope you're proud of me; I know I am. I love you all.

And of course, to my campaign supporters: Your contributions are what made my pipe dream of publishing a book into a reality. Thank you for everything you've done for me, both in this book journey and outside of it. I will never be able to thank you enough. Below are the names of my supporters.

Richard Yang

Carolyn Jiayi Chen

Carolyn Liu

Huachie Timothy Lee

Carolyn Liu

Freeman Su

Catherine Lee

Lillian B.L. Kuo

King Wu

Horace Wang

Lynne Greenberg

Ting-Hwa Tong

Sandra Shen

Jerry Chen

Claire Lin

Isabelle Chen

Ashley Sung

Frank Iovine

Hongrong Chen

Samantha Finley

Steph Shao

Jack Chen

Jasmine Chai

Ally Ick

Rauful Hossain

Andy Yang

Fanny Li

Shih-Chang Sheu

HsinLan Chen

Casey Barfield

Kenny Chiu

Melissa Rueda

Walter Chang

Hojung Lee

Chou YingChun

LiFen Liao

Trin Fan Chang

Grant West

Noor Lone

Pingyupan

Nelson Wu

Joan Sung

Lin Chih-Chia

Lisa Zhang

Leon Qu

Edward Sheu

Echo Xu

ShaoMei Pan

I-Wen Tsai

Audrey Moore

Gabrielle Luna

Nathan Chen

Ben Chen

Chien-Yin Sze

Kimberly Gail Tena

Max Kelbly

Sharon Young

Angela Chi

Crystal Chen

Gene Chen

James Muyskens

Andy Lopez

Emily Li

Miranda Lin

Grace Zhao

Elisabete Tien

Meg Chen

Nicole Cheng

Austin Chu

Ann Chiou

Joe Chang

Keng W. Tan

Karl Mulieri

Srinidhi Rao

Jordan Matuszewski

Eric Koester

Iram Rahman

Anthony V Doti

Alice Tsai

Sophia Newman

Christopher Chiang

Lisa Jackson

Kyle Michael Chacon

Yvonne Ma

Sophia Jin

Gang Zhang

Zhao Family

Janette Wu

Sarah Brys

Tong Liang

Michael Ruggiero

Ted Lin

Imei Hsiao

Content Warnings

UNHEALTHY RELATIONSHIPS